THE
DILEMMA
OF
EUROCOMMUNISM

THE LABOUR PARTY
1980

ISBN 0 86117 051 2
B/00780 Printed by Blackfriars Press Ltd., Leicester
and published by The Labour Party
144/152 Walworth Road, London SE17 1JT

CONTENTS

Foreword 5
Introduction 7
1 Italy: Eurocommunism's Pace-setter 14
2 France: Eurocommunism Amidst Uncertainty .. 30
3 Spain: Eurocommunism and Socialism 49
4 Eurocommunism: Conclusions 62

FOREWORD

This pamphlet, published by the Labour Party, arose out of work done by the National Executive Committee's Western Europe Sub-Committee which was set up in 1978. Building on our already strong links with our fraternal parties in Europe through the Socialist International, we are seeking to broaden the Labour Party's knowledge of and familiarity with the Left in Europe. The publication of this pamphlet on those European Communist Parties which profess democratic ideals and have substantial working class support, marks, we hope, a step in this direction.

Our thanks go to all those participating in the Sub-Committee which meets under the chairmanship of Eric Heffer MP, and particularly those contributing to this pamphlet: Percy Allum, David Bell, Stuart Holland, José Maravall, Edward Mortimer and Eric Shaw.

This paper is not a statement of party policy. The National Executive Committee has agreed that it be published in the belief that it will promote a reasoned and balanced approach to the issues raised.

Ron Hayward
January 1980   *General Secretary*

INTRODUCTION
by Eric Heffer MP

The Labour Party is an internationalist party. It is a member of the Socialist International, and is also a member of the Confederation of European Socialist Parties. Its record of support for the fighters for colonial freedom, as well as for those fighting oppression in capitalist and east European communist countries, is second to none. We want to see a democratic socialist Europe, as the first step towards a democratic socialist world, and this has come much closer because of events over recent years.

Britain's entry into the European Community has both negative and positive features. The EEC, with its Rome Treaty, is an organisation created to protect the capitalist system. For that basic reason, besides the heavy burden it places upon British people's shoulders, the Labour Party rejected entry into the Common Market, and argued for a 'No' vote decision in the 1975 referendum campaign. But the people decided by a majority to vote 'yes', and, despite our opposition to direct elections, once parliament decided to conduct them, we put forward candidates for the EEC Assembly, and today the Labour Party is represented there as part of the socialist group.

At the European Assembly there are other parties of the left, with the communists from France and Italy the most powerful. These, like the Spanish Communist Party, are termed Eurocommunists, a label not accepted by all of them, but, regardless of whether they like it or not, is likely to stick.

The Eurocommunist parties arose out of the situation which developed over the Soviet invasion of Czechoslovakia. A number of European communist parties simply could not accept the Soviet leaders' arguments, and increasingly distanced themselves from Soviet policies. In the process they have revised many of their theoretical concepts and fully accepted pluralism in politics, together with the democratic parliamentary path to socialism.

In this introduction I will concentrate, in particular, on the attitude, as I understand it, which the British Labour Party adopts towards the Eurocommunists. I will also say something about its relationship with the communist parties of eastern Europe and the Soviet Union, that is, those which have political state power. The question of its relationships with communist parties does not loom large in the discussions or thinking of the British Labour Party. This is not because of lack of general interest, but due to two very good reasons. First, the British Communist Party is electorally insignificant — and, therefore, of no electoral importance — and in many respects is being outflanked on the left by small parties and groups. Secondly, as Labour is often in government, relationships with governmental communist parties tend to be looked at with one eye on the diplomatic consequences, and whether visits and discussions are in the interests of the Labour government of the day. Such contacts with such communist parties are thus largely in connection with foreign policy interests.

I am not saying that the party's attitude is entirely determined by the interests of a Labour government, but, undoubtedly, this is a factor which is seriously considered.

There is also a third reason, which is that the British Labour Party, a loyal member of the Socialist International, at no time wishes to act independently, or against the interests of its fellow international members. That is why, although it invited the Italian, French and Spanish communist parties — the main Eurocommunists — to send official observers to its 1978 and 1979 annual conferences, it nevertheless first sounded its Socialist International colleagues to find out whether this would embarrass them, or their comrades in the three countries concerned.

With regard to the communist parties in the countries where they have power, formal exchange visits between cultural organisations etc and the Labour Party have taken place. Such exchanges have often been criticised by reactionary forces in Britain, which have deliberately misrepresented their motives. These exchanges are primarily designed as cultural or goodwill visits, and do not go beyond an exchange of views, usually ending with joint statements stressing the cultural and other interests of both organisations and countries concerned. Such discussions are designed to assist the development of détente, whilst in no way accepting the political concepts or objectives of each organisation concerned.

With regard to the three Eurocommunist parties which were asked to attend Labour conferences, it was hoped that from such visits Labour could discover just how far the Eurocommunists had gone, how far their views were strategic and not tactical, and whether in the future further exchanges of views would be useful, both to the Labour Party — especially now Britain is part of the Common Market — and to the International. At Labour's conferences there were no formal discussions. All were informally held between individuals.

Could it be said the discussions were fruitful? Only time will tell. But if one is concerned with socialist and democratic development in Europe, then the Eurocommunists cannot be ignored.

The question of vital importance is: are these communist parties really sincere? How far have they gained independence from Moscow? And just how far have they jettisoned their earlier intellectual baggage, which has made genuine co-operation between communists and socialists in the past almost impossible?

Socialists are naturally suspicious whether their statements are only tactical when they look at the campaign waged by French communists against French socialists before the French general election. This is so despite the fact that the left of the French Socialist Party is fairly close in its policies to the French Communist Party. The French campaign brings to mind the statement by Ponomarov, quoted by Professor Ehmke, the West German socialist, when he said in July 1975 that communists must 'never forget their independent class position for a moment, and not abstain from serious, justifiable criticism of social democratism as the ideology and practice of co-operation between the classes'. One is entitled to ask, therefore, how far the French Communist Party is influenced by Moscow's thinking, and how far it is taking an independent line. It is possible that more dogmatic forces are reasserting themselves. Again, only time will tell.

However, it would be wrong to believe the position of the Eurocommunists is purely tactical. I accept what Santiago Carrillo, the Spanish Communist Party leader, says in his book *Eurocommunism and the State*: 'The Eurocommunist phenomenon is not a tactical manoeuvre . . . It is an autonomous strategic conception in the process of formation, born of the experience of those concerned and of concrete reality'.

It is, as Professor Ehmke says, 'of some importance in the long term that even communists now admit the inherent value of the basic rights and political freedoms of bourgeois democracy'.

The acceptance of democracy, religious freedom, plurality of political parties, an independent trade union movement, a free press, freedom of opinion, free and democratic universal suffrage, is of immense importance. These are rights which had to be fought for. They were not handed to the labour movement as a gift from God. Every freedom in a bourgeois society is in reality a measure of workers' freedom. They are freedoms which have to be defended and extended at all times, often in the face of bitterly hostile reactionary elements.

Czechoslovakia

It cannot be an accident that it was in Czechoslovakia that 'socialism with a human face' was fought for. Czechoslovakia had known a democratic bourgeois society, which was first destroyed by Nazism, restored briefly at the end of the war, and later again destroyed in the name of socialism. Why should those who had known free discussions, and been able to exchange ideas freely, then meekly accept Soviet tutelage and thought control without trying to reverse the process?

There is no doubt the invasion of Czechoslovakia by the Warsaw Pact countries, excluding Romania, was traumatic for communists seeking to rid themselves of the Stalinist image and concepts. The effect of the Czechoslovak situation was graphically explained by Carrillo when he wrote: 'For us, for the Communist Party of Spain, the culminating point in winning our independence was the occupation of Czechoslovakia in 1968. The preparations for that operation had been carried out with methods similar to those employed in the famous trials in 1936, which had been exposed at the 20th Congress of the Communist Party of the Soviet Union, or similar to those used in the denunciation of Yugoslavia in 1946. That is to say, a bold statement was made — in this case that Czechoslovakia was on the verge of falling into the hands of capitalism — and with that statement as a starting point, stories were concocted that were light years away from the truth. This was far more than we could be expected to swallow. Czechoslovakia was the straw which broke the camel's back, and led our parties to say "no". That kind of "internationalism" had come to an end as far as we were concerned.'

I was on holiday on the Isle of Elba when the Warsaw Pact countries, under Soviet leadership, occupied Czechoslovakia. I learned of the attack, and the Italian Communist Party's opposition to it, from a notice board outside the CP headquarters on the island. The Italian CP, like the Spanish, could not accept the arguments being advanced by the Warsaw Pact countries. For them, as for the Spanish, this so-called internationalism was not acceptable.

This was an advance on the situation which existed in the communist parties over Hungary. True, members left the party in large numbers. But, in the main, the leadership of the CPs went along with the Soviet explanations. Not so with regard to Czechoslovakia. The Khruschev revelations undoubtedly began the first stage of the end of Soviet control.

The truth, which had often been alleged in Trotskyist, bourgeois and socialist papers, about Stalinist brutality was now officially revealed. No longer could the stories of concentration camps and police methods to deal with dissent, of the suppression of all opposition, of the false and phoney trials, be brushed aside as so much capitalist propaganda. At last the truth was revealed, and this meant that every statement from that time onwards out of the Soviet Union could no longer be taken on its face value. The beginning of Eurocommunism had its roots in the querying of the actual political system of the Soviet Union by Palmiro Togliatti, the Italian Communist leader. It was he who raised the question of the system of state power being wrong, and argued that from that time onwards the communist world would have a number of centres — not just one. He developed the concept of 'polycentrism'. The Yugoslav communists had made the initial stand, then the Chinese disagreement developed, then there were the Kruschev revelations, the Polish Spring, the Hungarian uprising and ultimately Czechoslovakia. It was quite clear the situation in the communist world could never be the same.

Centrifugal forces had always been there, but now the prestige of the Soviet Union was badly battered. It was impossible for its leaders to reassert their total authority, except by force, and that they could only do when they had military control, as in the Warsaw Pact countries.

The question for socialists was which way would the communist parties outside Soviet control jump? In their bid for independence would they move towards leftist, perhaps Trotskyist, positions, or towards the type of Marxist concepts which existed in the social democratic parties prior to the First World War? Would they split into right-left factions?

There have been splits. There have been groups who have gone Trotskyist. Others have adhered to Maoist ideology. Others have joined social democratic and labour parties. But, generally, they have remained remarkably solid, yet with a confused position, especially towards the Soviet Union. Many wish to be independent of the Soviet Union, though not to break entirely with it. In some cases they argue that the Soviet Union is a genuinely socialist country, but a model which they do not wish to follow. It is because the situation is a developing one that I believe it is essential for socialists to carry out a dialogue with the Eurocommunists so they can be further influenced and strengthened in their democratic socialist concepts.

Degree of Change

For our part, we must be prepared to admit that social democratic parties and governments, and socialists generally, have not always been as positively socialist as they could have been. Too often, western socialists have appeared as but one further type of administration of the capitalist system, or as supporters of US policy, rather than politicians based on the working class, dedicated to ending that system. Today that situation is undoubtedly undergoing a degree of change. Under pressure of events, with a resuscitation of ideas and also growth of the youth movement, the socialist parties have taken a more left position, and that process, like the process of democratisation in the communist parties, is still going on.

As Giorgio Napolitano says in the book *The Italian Road to Socialism*, the situation is complex. He puts it this way: 'We communists, supposedly, have done no more of late than to have arrived twenty years behind time, at the same conclusions reached by the Socialist Party at the end of the 1950s. But this is a polemical simplification that doesn't hold. The journey of both of our parties has been far more complex. Our Leninist matrix, and our concern to conserve the maximum rigour in formulating our positions of principle, have helped us from slipping into politically dangerous attitudes and behaviour, but they have not prevented us from undergoing courageous innovations in the development of theory, strategic positions and political ideas.'

What Attitude?

Therefore, what attitude should socialists take towards the Eurocommunist parties. First, it is important that they look at the objective political situation in their own country, and in Europe. If the CPs accept the democratic process, if they have declared independence from the Soviet Union, even a limited one, if they are prepared to accept pluralism, then, providing they have a mass base, it is obvious that agreements should be discussed, and, if necessary, entered into. This was a perfectly correct tactic for the French Socialist Party to adopt, as it is for the Italian Socialist Party to enter into agreements to administer Italy's cities and municipalities. In the process, further discussions can take place. In fact, it may at times be necessary to combat the innate conservatism of the Eurocommunists, who, under certain circumstances, look more gradualist than Britain's Fabian Society. A simple British saying is that there should be 'horses for courses'. This, I feel, applies to the Eurocommunist parties.

It is essential that if discussions take place they should centre on the ideological issues, and equally the organisational one. It is conceivable that out of this, in certain countries, a new, regenerated movement can arise. I personally accept the statement of Santiago

Carrillo when he wrote in *Eurocommunism and the State* that 'there is no reason for not healing the split . . . and arriving at a convergence on the basis of scientific socialism and democracy'. This, however, can only be done on the basis of common objectives and common policies, freely arrived at. The best way for agreement is, where necessary, electoral agreement. This is necessary in Italy and France, and it could be necessary in the European Parliamentary Assembly so that limited objectives could be attained.

On the other hand, if CPs have no electoral base, it would be foolish for socialists to help them create one. This is not being anti-Eurocommunist. It is being non-Eurocommunist. Certainly such a policy must be the one for Britain. Equally it is true of some other European countries.

One other aspect of the Eurocommunist situation is the question of détente, and the attitude to be adopted towards the communist parties of the Soviet Union and the East European states. Discussions and exchange visits are only useful to help create peaceful international conditions. They must not be allowed to be used for propaganda purposes, so that an impression is given internally, and to the world, that socialist parties approve of the undemocratic nature of those states. In fact, when exchange visits take place, it is the duty and responsibility of socialists from western parties to explain clearly their attitude on human rights, on the socialist concept of freedom, and to show solidarity with those in communist countries who seek freedom and democracy. They should clearly say they support those communists and socialists who signed the Charter 77 in Czechoslovakia. They should show their solidarity with people like Zdenek Mlyner, who wrote a letter to communist and socialist parties on 16 January 1977, in which he said: 'I am a communist who is convinced that socialism must give the people a larger measure of political and civil rights, and liberation, than capitalism.'

They should support, in particular, the Medvedev brothers and other Soviet Union dissidents who do not want a return to capitalism, but seek democracy. The book by Roy Medvedev on socialist democracy is a model of socialist thought. We should tell the Soviet, East German, Polish, Czech and other CP leaders that as long as they refuse democracy, whilst we seek to live in peace with them, we cannot be expected to go beyond that. As some Eurocommunist leaders have said, the supposed socialism of the communist countries has done untold harm to the cause of socialism. That has to be said, and for socialists there can be no compromise on that question, and no double standards.

Socialists must reject the bureaucratic societies of the communist countries and equally, the unbridled, competitive, capitalist systems of western Europe. We must strive to plan our resources sensibly, but with democratic control and freedom. If public ownership is extended, it must be with democratic management, so that bureaucracy cannot take over, becoming an even greater parasitic growth on society than monopoly capitalism.

It is to these problems that we must address ourselves. Merely to become socialist governments, without seeking to fundamentally change society, is essentially a betrayal of our socialist objectives.

The British Labour Party's programme, carried at its 1976 conference, says: 'Our programme is founded on the principles of democracy and socialism. At its heart is a basic socialist priority — to bring about a fundamental and irreversible shift in the balance of power and wealth, in favour of working people and their families.'

We believe this can best be done by the public ownership of the means of production, distribution and exchange, under democratic control by the workers of hand and brain. If we fight to carry out that sort of policy, then Eurocommunism cannot win the workers' support away from the socialists. Eventually they will have to come to us, and, together, a regenerated socialist movement in Europe will emerge.

In conclusion, I think we should heed the words of Otto Bauer, the Austrian social democratic leader, who, in 1935, said to Ernst Fischer, the Austrian communist (and I think it is of importance today in deciding our position vis-a-vis the Eurocommunists):

'To jump from one embankment to the other is not enough. We must build a solid and lasting bridge. Some from one side, others from the other side. One and the same bridge, starting from both embankments.'

I hope this pamphlet will be part of the bridge building.

1 ITALY: EUROCOMMUNISM'S PACE-SETTER

Eurocommunism has been most frequently associated with the Italian Communist Party (PCI). It is the largest Communist party in the western world, the second largest party in Italy, and the most articulate and consistent exponent of those ideas and attitudes which are now regarded as defining characteristics of 'Eurocommunism'. Finally, of all Communist parties in western Europe, it is the one which has come closest to the threshhold of power. It can be either feared or admired — but it cannot be ignored.

Initially, the PCI was reluctant to use the term 'Eurocommunism'. This reflected its hesitation to claim adherence to — or even parentage of — a new type of communism, clearly distinct from the Soviet variety. The party had, since 1956, if not earlier, upheld the right of each communist party to decide its own road to socialism and act independently of any controlling centre. Palmiro Togliatti, long-time leader of the PCI, advocated *'Unity in Diversity'* in the world communist movement, in place of the Stalinist ideal of a monolith, directed from the Kremlin. But precisely because Italian communists insisted on national autonomy, and the need for each communist party to develop its policies in the light of particular national traditions and circumstances, they were reluctant to embrace a new type of communism, which, implicitly, had a general, transnational, rather than a uniquely national relevance. After all, Togliatti could claim that the pursuit of diverse roads to socialism, in which Italy's would differ from Russia's, was no more than taking Stalin's 'Socialism in one country' to its logical conclusion. In the same way, it represented no obvious challenge to Soviet-style communism. One could propagate a specifically Italian-style communism, meeting Italy's own national requirements, while re-affirming that Moscow's communism was finely cut to suit Russian cloth. Santiago Carrillo, leader of the Spanish Communist Party (PCE), was the first to throw caution to the winds and proudly adopt the Eurocommunist label. Eurocommunism, he claimed, offered not only a *different road* to socialism, but a *superior model* of socialism. He then went on to express doubts about the Soviet Union's right to call itself socialist at all.

The PCI has, so far, been more cautious. Nevertheless, it has now significantly accepted the Eurocommunist label. Eurocommunism, it argues, embodies a new form of communism, with its own distinct characteristics, which amount to more than an adaptation to local traditions and needs. As such, it can be conceived as an alternative model to Soviet-style communism. Thus, the PCI's *'Draft Theses'* prepared for the party's 1979 congress state:

> 'In recent years, the Italian communists' thinking has met with similar, but autonomous reasoning on the part of other communist parties in Western Europe, and in countries such as Japan. Despite the historical differences and diversities in orientation under which they operate, these parties have arrived at the common conviction that the fight for

socialism and the building of socialism must take place within the context of full expansion of democracy and all freedoms. This is the option of Eurocommunism.'

While the PCI denies that Eurocommunism offers a 'universally valid' solution, it clearly conceives it to be the socialism of the developed world. The next step forward — one which the party has not yet taken — is to present it as the most developed form of socialism. This would constitute an explicit challenge to Moscow — hence, doubtless, the PCI's prudence.

The PCI and Democracy

Much western comment on the PCI is concentrated on the sincerity of its protestations of faith in democracy. Can it be trusted to govern, or participate in governing Italy, without subverting its democratic institutions?

Originally, the newly-founded communist parties, in the years after the Russian revolution, sharply distinguished themselves from their socialist rivals by their scepticism, or even outright hostility to 'bourgeois democracy'. Instead, they espoused the notion of 'the dictatorship of the proletariat' — a term which had far less in common with what Marx meant when he infrequently used it, than with Soviet political practice. The history of the development of Eurocommunism has been its gradual jettisoning of the notion of the dictatorship of the proletariat, or, in real terms, its distancing itself from Soviet political practice.

The PCI asserts that the Bolshevik experience is not relevant to the political circumstances of modern western Europe. Its leader, Enrico Berlinguer, emphasised, in a report to the central committee in October 1975, that it was 'totally unrealistic to take the strategy and tactics of the great Russian revolutions of 1917, or even 1905, as guidelines for the political struggle of the proletariat in the west today'. It was, he continued, 'unthinkable that socialism can be built in the west in the forms and ways in which it was achieved in the Soviet Union and in other countries of eastern Europe and Asia'.[2] The PCI, in fact, is rejecting two types of strategies for achieving socialism — the Leninist concept of a seizure of power by a well-organised revolutionary elite, albeit with mass support and, more generally, any form of revolutionary socialism. A party can be revolutionary without being Leninist, as Rosa Luxembourg insisted. The PCI is neither. Insofar as a chief dividing point between social democratic parties and the communist breakaway factions after 1918 was over the desirability and practicality of the parliamentary road to socialism, the PCI has most emphatically, in the circumstances it now finds itself, moved into the former camp. Indeed, somewhat ironically, one can argue that the Eurocommunists, in their firmly-held and oft-reiterated conviction that socialism — understood as radically changed social and economic arrangements, rather than as a source of rhetorical slogans — can be attained by electoral means, are far closer to the spirit and doctrine of classical social democracy than are the contemporary claimants to that name.

The PCI's full conversion to the parliamentary road to socialism reflects the acceptance of western political principles and institutions. Thus, a joint Italian and French communist statement, issued in November 1975, declares that 'all the freedoms — which are a product of the great democratic bourgeois revolution, and of the great popular struggles of this century, headed by the working class — will have to be guaranteed and developed. This holds true for freedom of thought and expression, freedom of the press, of assembly, association and demonstration, free movement of persons inside and outside their country, the inviolability of private life, religious freedom, and total freedom of expression for currents of thought and every philosophical, cultural and artistic opinion'. The two parties reaffirmed their support 'for the plurality of political parties, for the right to existence and activity of opposition parties for the free formation of majorities and minorities and the possibility of their alternating democratically . . . for independence of the judiciary . . . for the freedom of activity and autonomy of the trade unions'.[3] The sincerity of these sentiments has been widely accepted by the PCI's political opponents. Thus no less a staunch and veteran anti-communist than Giuseppe Saragat, ex-President of Italy and former leader of the Social Democratic Party (PSDI) — formed as an anti-communist, right-wing splinter from the Nenni-led Italian Socialist Party, with British and American help, in 1948 — has stated clearly that he has 'no doubts about the communists' credibility as a democratic party', a point of view shared by Umberto Agnelli, deputy chairman of Fiat.[4]

The PCI's attachment to western democracy, as currently practised, is, however, by no means unqualified. It is regarded as a partial and insufficient form of democracy. Communist spokesmen emphasise that if the promise of democracy is to be fulfilled, one must widen and foster the opportunity and ability of ordinary people to determine the decisions and circumstances which shape their lives. Thus one communist MP defined democracy as 'that form where the citizen participates in as broad a way as possible in all the problems of society — not just called to vote once every five years, and then he minds his own business, and others act for him . . . In the end, democracy is the participation of everyone in all problems'.[5] Nor is this mere rhetoric. In the regions where the PCI has long controlled local government — the so-called red belt of Emilia-Romagna, Umbria and Tuscany — the party has actively sought to engage as many interests and people as possible in the political process. Furthermore, the PCI holds that democracy cannot be restricted to the political sphere, but must extend to the workplace.

As Marxists, Italian communists also approach democracy from a class viewpoint. But their object is not some so-called dictatorship of the proletariat, but the reduction of the power and wealth of ruling groups in the interests of the working masses. In the socialist transformation they envisage, they call for — in Berlinguer's words — 'the rise to national leadership of the workers, allied with all the other productive forces of society, and their effective participation in the management of economic and political life'.[6]

Some western observers, like Henry Kissinger, remain unconvinced by communist declarations of support for political democracy, seeing them as snares to trap the unwary. One prominent Italian political leader, the late Ugo La Malfa, a former highly respected President of the Republican Party and Deputy Prime Minister when he died in the spring of 1979, addressed himself to Kissinger's line of argument. In an article published shortly before his death, he wrote that, to present a convincing case 'doomwatchers' like Kissinger have to assert that 'every word the Eurocommunists have uttered is just part of an intricate, cunning scheme to get into power, and, once there, to lose no time on setting up a totalitarian regime'.[7]

In reality, La Malfa argued, considerable evidence suggested that the PCI leaders were genuinely committed to parliamentary democracy. Why else 'embark on a long, soul-searching reappraisal of its ideologies and policies', simply to cast all this work aside at a suitable moment? Why also, as Berlinguer has done, defend pluralism and western democracy before an important, but unreceptive audience in Moscow, on the occasion of the 60th anniversary of the October revolution? Leaving aside the sincerity of the communist leadership's intention, La Malfa also reasons that an attempt to overthrow Italy's democratic system was doomed to failure, and would antagonise many PCI sympathisers who had rallied behind the party, precisely because it presented itself as a champion of democracy.[8]

Evidence that support for democracy is widespread in communist ranks was supplied by a study of the beliefs of Italian party members. Based on research carried out a decade ago, before the PCI's adoption of the historic compromise, the study found that 'Most communists . . . are classical democrats . . . Authoritarian democrats are concentrated in the Christian Democratic Party.'[9]

The same author commented on a more recent work that 'all the available evidence supports the conclusion that if advocacy of mass participation in politics and hostility to elitism in government be the only criteria, the communists are the most democratic force in Italy'.[10]

PCI Party Structure

The PCI, nevertheless, does not carry its enthusiasm for participatory democracy over to its own internal workings. This does not mean that the PCI is organised along totalitarian lines. Absence of fully democratic forms and practices does not necessarily imply a rigid and authoritarian structure — as some critics of the PCI readily assume. No one has ever held up the Conservative Party as a model of democratic organisation. But nor, whatever its other failings, can it be accused of being autocratic in structure.

Thus for most western world parties, internal democracy is not a quality which is either present or absent, but something which exists to varying degrees. But before measuring the extent of intra-party democracy in the PCI, it is necessary to define the term. Ideally, intra-party democracy would describe that state of affairs where the party officers are elected at all stages; where policy formation lies in the hands of democratically elected bodies; where leaders and MPs are subject to regular re-selection procedures; and where all significant policy or strategic decisions made reflect the will of most members.

Simply to describe this ideal state of affairs is to demonstrate that it is infrequently to be found in real life. Hence the question to be asked is to what extent the PCI approximates, in its forms and practices, a democratically-run party?

The basic units within the party are cells, located at the workplace, and sections, which are geographical. Each is combined into federations. Above the federation is the supreme party body, the national congress, which elects the 177-member central committee. This, in turn, elects the directorate of 25 members and the most powerful body, the nine-member secretariat.

All executive bodies are, in Leninist fashion, responsible to their superiors, at least as much as to those who elect them. Similarly, the various electorates — cells, sections, federations or congress — are not free to elect whom they choose. They are presented with lists, which are sanctioned by the next body up in the hierarchy. For example, the retiring central committee has to give its seal of approval to lists of candidates for the next central committee presented to congress. In recent years the tendency has been to allow more freedom of choice at each stage. It is likely that a good deal of democracy and accountability to members now exists at lower levels.

The classic Leninist-type party is one organised in small, tightly-controlled workplace cells, structured in a vertical and not horizontal manner, to discourage the development of opposition factions. Recently, in the PCI, the number of cells has fallen considerably. The party is now largely organised in sections, which generally coincide with local government boundaries, might contain over 1,000 members, and meet only every two months. Within sections, and in the remaining cells, differences of opinion and criticisms of party decisions on a wide range of matters — in particular, recently, on economic and labour relations problems — are now more and more common. Frequent modifications in the party's complex organisational structure have weakened the chain of command, making it ever more difficult for the leadership to control the rank and file. Similarly, there are growing horizontal contacts between PCI activists and office-holders, which intensify party management problems and facilitate the growth of distinct local tendencies.

Given these developments, a comment by one student of western communist parties is apposite. 'Plainly, this is the transition [within the PCI] from the Leninist party, with its cells, to the ordinary party, with its constituency groups — that is from a party based on militancy to one based on electoralism.'[11] In the south, the process has been taken one stage further — or rather the party has evolved in a different direction. It has taken on some of the characteristics of the Christian Democratic party in the south in that to a significant extent it is controlled by local party notables able to disburse patronage, and therefore command support. The PCI membership, then, does not decide either the process of policy formation or leadership selection, though it may influence both those who control the party machine and those who have the major say on how the party is run and what it does. But this control is exercised increasingly in an indirect and subtle, rather than a crude manner.

Thus, the leadership is elected, but in fact it manages elections. A system of co-option operates, based on the career patterns of party officials. The Communist Party is the only Italian party which acts as a vehicle of social promotion of the proletarian classes. A political career for a person of modest origin means becoming a full-time official. Entry into the national leadership is possible only for those who reach office-holding positions at provincial level; and three-quarters of provincial officials, regardless of social origin, are full-time, paid career men. Since the party apparatus is in the hands of people whose livelihood depends on their party career, it is easy to see how the party leadership can control the apparatus.

The PCI's parliamentary group, now numbering 228 from a total of 630 deputies, is subordinated to the party leadership. Whilst top leaders are often deputies, their power derives from their position in the party hierarchy — in particular, membership of the directorate and the secretariat. Strict party discipline ensures that MPs conform to party decisions. They have little freedom of action in opposition to the party leadership.[12] It should, however, be understood that the leadership does not constitute a monolithic group, under firm, centralised direction. It includes different viewpoints, which are debated freely — in inner party circles at least.

The PCI claims to abide by the principles of democratic centralism. This it differentiates from the autocratic, bureaucratic centralism to be found in the Soviet bloc parties. It may be useful to set down here the definition of democratic centralism offered by Antonio Gramsci, the party's revered former leader and theoretician, which, PCI leaders assert, govern the mode of internal operation of the party. Gramsci explained his conception of democratic centralism as 'a continual adaptation of the organisation to the real movement, a matching of thrusts from below, with orders from above, a continuous insertion of elements thrown up from the depths of the rank and file into the solid framework of the leadership apparatus, which ensures continuity and the regular accumulation of experience'.[13] It will be noted that the definition emphasises the leadership's responsiveness to the rank and file, rather than direct and full accountability to it. This conception of democratic centralism is gradually coming to characterise the actual workings of the PCI. It is not a state of affairs which exists at present, but the trend appears to be in this direction.

Insofar as the party is democratic, then it is so in the 'vanguard' rather than 'mass party' sense. Here it bears the stamp of its origins. But the PCI is constantly evolving in structure, as well as strategy, and it may well be drifting away from the vanguard model as it becomes more integrated into the political structure of the country.

It is, however, superficial to contrast the PCI's actual functioning with an idealised version of a democratic party structure, to be rarely, if at all, found in any major party. For this reason, another yardstick of democracy, frequently applied, is the extent to which a party tolerates the open expression of diverse strands of opinion. Party leaders are apt to contrast the PCI, well-disciplined and coherently-organised, with the faction-ridden nature of all other parties, including the PSI. These factions are partly ideological, but also reliant on the powers of patronage acquired by various party notables — the so-called clientele system. However, this, in a way, evades the issue — which is, does the party permit a plurality of viewpoints, can they be articulated openly, and are they allowed to compete freely for support? No conclusive answer can be given to these questions. Some things are, nevertheless, clear. The party is not monolithic. Different strands of opinion do exist, and are recognised as such. The party leadership, unlike its French Communist Party counterpart, has permitted open and critical discussion of the PCI ideology and history. Since the 1976 elections there has been a spirited and sometimes divisive debate within the party over the problems of unemployment, inflation and wage restraint and, more generally, on the terms on which the PCI would collaborate with the ruling Christian Democrats. The debate is continuing, and, if anything, intensifying in volume and vigour, especially after the party's serious setback in the 1979 general election.

Though the leadership is not democratically responsible to the rank and file, it does have to take account of its state of mind. It is not insensitive to strong currents of opinion running contrary to official party policy. Twice, it appears that it retreated from positions it had adopted, under pressure from the rank and file — first, over the support it was prepared to give to the Andreotti government's incomes policy, and, secondly, over the conditions on which it was willing to maintain that government in power. In short, party activists cannot dictate party policy, but they can set limits to the range of options and scope for manoeuvre open to the leadership.

Finally, the PCI is increasingly an open party, exposed to outside influences and pressure group activity, and far from the classic communist party, insulated from the world outside. The largely communist union federation, the CGIL, is gradually developing into an autonomous body rather than the vehicle for mobilizing working class support of traditional communist strategy, and its leaders exercise an independent influence within the PCI leadership. The party also arranges conferences with intellectuals, religious, business and political leaders of varying political complexion. Whilst it seeks to influence these groups, there is every reason to believe that it is a two-way process. The CGIL leadership, in turn, is increasingly subject to shop floor pressure, due to the rapid growth in strength and vigour of the shop steward movement in the last decade. This means that the communist trade union leadership no longer has the ability — even if it had the desire — to act as a transmission belt for orders from the party to the workplace.

PCI — Domestic Policies

The domestic economic policies of the PCI, in particular, have attracted criticism from both right and left, in Italy and abroad. On the one hand, certain PSI leaders have claimed recently to discern a return by the PCI to aggressively radical policies. On the other hand, in complete contrast, both domestic and foreign observers have argued that, for example, in its attitudes towards public ownership, and in its emphasis on consensual politics, the PCI has effectively adopted a social democratic position. Clearly, these criticisms are mutually exclusive, though not necessarily equally misguided.

The PCI emphatically rejects the idea of a totally state-controlled and bureaucratically planned economy. Indeed, it accepts the continued survival of a flourishing private sector in the foreseeable future. Thus Giorgio Napolitano, the party's senior economic spokesman, affirmed 'the role of private initiative, and even large-scale private industry, (and) the function of profit and the market economy'.[14] In sharp contrast with the French Communist Party, and French Socialist Party for that matter, the PCI envisages no widespread extension of public ownership. This partly reflects the considerable size and range of the existing public sector in industry, banking and insurance, in Italy. The PCI argues that the existing public sector enterprises — para-statal corporations like the IRI and ENI, and state-owned banks and financial institutions — can be deployed as efficient instruments of economic planning.

Once they are reorganised, freed from corruption and political favouritism, and attuned to social objectives, they are well capable of guiding the economy as a whole into desired directions. The PCI reasons that market forces alone have proved incapable of creating sustained economic expansion, and of meeting the economic and social aspirations of working people. However, the type of planning the communists have in mind differs considerably from the Soviet-style command economy. The party's medium-term economic programme states that planning will guarantee, through the selection of priorities and the establishment of balance, 'an increased capacity for innovation and competitiveness in the Italian economy . . . and especially guarantee the development of small firms and co-operatives'.[15]

According to communist economic thinking, both planning and the market have their special functions to perform. A correct balance between them must be struck, in order to achieve 'the greatest efficiency in execution of the goals of planning itself, together with maximum degree of dynamism and innovation.[16]

The PCI invites the co-operation of privately-owned firms. Napolitano sees as the 'characteristic feature' of the party's programme 'its refusal to abandon economic development to spontaneous activity, its insistence on democratic control of the uses of the "surplus", and in the guidance given by democratic public powers to social and economic transformation'.[17]

In contrast to the French Communist Party, the PCI does not believe that the transformation of class relations in society is effectively accomplished by nationalisation alone. In the latter's view, state ownership by itself does not guarantee that labour supplants capital as the dominant force in society. By also proposing workers' control in industry, the PCI recognises the danger of the emergence of a state capitalist, or bureaucratic collectivist, rather than a socialist society.

In other aspects of economic and financial policy, the PCI's approach is characterised by caution and an unwillingness to consider sharp alterations of course. Party spokesmen have praised the 'sensible' monetary policy practised by the Bank of Italy. On trade policy, protectionist measures to remedy Italy's recurrent balance of payments problems have been rejected in favour of government-inspired industrial reorganisation to improve the competitiveness of Italian exports.

It should be added that whilst the PCI's economic policies have been welcomed by Keynesian economists, left-wing critics have detected major flaws. They doubt whether the redirection of economic and social goals can be achieved in a plan which relies so much on co-operation with private enterprise. Two possibilities, they argue, will then open. Either the party, if it achieves a place in government, will be forced to water down its policies for social and structural reforms, or private enterprise will resist attempts to tamper with its dynamic — perhaps with an investment strike, and flight of capital abroad. Certainly, one must agree that industry and finance in western Europe has frequently shown itself allergic to the mildest attempts to introduce some form of planning.

PCI Political Strategy

The PCI's strategy is of particular interest to socialists in western Europe because it treats, with an issue of overriding concern, how can socialism be built in a modern, developed capitalist system while avoiding the pitfalls of violent upheaval and mild reformism which leave the basic institutions of capitalist society untouched.

The PCI's present political strategy — the so-called historic compromise — represents not a sudden switch in its thinking, but the outcome of a long process of rethinking the problems of the transition to socialism. In 1944, returning from exile in the Soviet Union, the PCI leader, Togliatti, formulated the communist response to the collapse of fascism. He called for the unity of all popular anti-fascist forces and the establishment of a progressive, democratic republic. Italy would remain capitalist, but the working class would be a major political force in it. Indeed, from 1944 until 1947, the country was governed by a coalition of Christian Democrats, communists and socialists. While in government, the PCI pursued a cautious policy, making no attempt to bring about fundamental social change.

Togliatti's strategy presupposed a long period of collaboration between the three major forces in Italian society — the Catholic, the socialist and the communist — in establishing a progressive democratic republic. These pre-conditions were shattered by the rapid onset of the Cold War in 1946-47, which led to the expulsion of the Communist Party from the government in summer 1947, and the Christian Democrat electoral landslide of 18 April 1948. Despite these setbacks, the Communist Party did not withdraw into a sectarian Stalinist shell. It kept its bridges open, collaborated in the drafting of the republican constitution, and in parliament, when its non co-operation could have paralysed constitutional government in Italy. This policy was pursued with tenacity — and some confusion, it must be added —

throughout the Cold War, and, expanded in the post-Stalinist thaw, saw it make modest electoral gains in the 50s, more substantial ones in the 60s, and the breakthrough, or perhaps more appropriately, the breakout, of 1975-76.

The historic compromise is the latest phase in the PCI's steadily evolving strategy. It represents, thus, not a sharp break — rather a significant shift in thinking, and an adaptation to changing conditions. Berlinguer launched the proposal for an historic compromise — that is, an alliance between the three principal forces in Italian society, the communist, Christian Democratic and socialist — in autumn 1973. Its relevance only becomes clear if it is taken in the context of two events. The first was the fate of Dubcek in Czechoslovakia in 1968, and the second was the dramatic overthrow of Allende's socialist experiment in Chile in 1973. Both demonstrated the limits to socialist advance in east and west. Berlinguer concluded that it was illusory to think socialist advances could be made on the basis of a narrow electoral victory. These would only be possible if they had the support of the greater part of the Italian people.

The overthrow of Allende bit deeply into the consciousness of many PCI leaders, because they detected the existence in Italian society of many ingredients of the Chilean tragedy. They saw a real possibility of a fascist, or authoritarian, right-wing resurgence, if an alliance were to be fashioned from among the representatives of big capital, reactionary political elements in the Army, secret service, Carabinieri — well-armed and well-trained semi-military police — and the civil service plus, providing a mass social base, a discontented and fearful section of the lower middle class. Berlinguer and others were gravely disturbed at the prospect of a sharp polarisation between right and left, if the left attempted to govern alone. They believe that Allende made a major mistake in not trying to conciliate the Christian Democratic Party in Chile — a mistake they intend to avoid.

The PCI's political strategy is sometimes defined in terms of a move from conflict or oppositional politics to a more consensual approach. This, in turn, is seen as a step towards the social-democratisation of the party. According to this view, the Italian communists no longer adhere to a strict class model of society, and, like the social democratic parties of northern Europe, believe that piecemeal reforms can be implemented on the basis of a wide measure of consent, and with the electoral support or approval of middle and lower-middle class social groups. Depending on the standpoint of the observer, this shift in attitude is either welcomed as a triumph for reason and moderation, or denounced as a betrayal of socialism and the working class.

This view is, however, over-simplified. The PCI, itself, claims to be pursuing a 'third road', distinct from both traditional communist and social democratic politics. The party's rejection of the former has already been documented. It also repudiates the charge of having become a social democratic or Labour party. The party leadership is sensitive to criticism of having 'sold out', and wants to reaffirm its commitment to radical social change. But there are other grounds for treating with caution the 'communist-social democratic' duality as a means of describing the party's present strategy. It overlooks two key ideas, derived from Antonio Gramsci, the early leader and noted theorist of the PCI, which Italian communists claim guide their conduct. The first is the concept of 'hegemony'.

Gramsci distinguished between two sources of authority in society — domination and hegemony. By domination, he meant the use of traditional instruments of state power — the army, police etc — to maintain control. Gramsci used the term hegemony to describe the cultural ascendancy of a ruling class — that is, the widespread and general acceptance by subordinate social groups of the morality, attitudes, ideas and aspirations of the dominant social class. This, he felt, was a more effective way of preserving the status quo, because it implied the consent of the masses of the right to rule, the superior qualities and particular moral and intellectual virtues of the privileged classes in society. He concluded that the working class, in order to gain power, must supplant the hegemony of the bourgeoisie by developing and propagating its own distinctive culture or ideology, which must be equally broad in scope, and appeal to all suppressed social groups. Socialism, or Marxism, could, in this way, equip the working class with the moral leadership in society, and rally behind its banner the vast majority of people in society. In Gramsci's words, 'a social group can, and indeed must, already exercise leadership, before winning governmental power'.[18]

The PCI, which regards itself as the organised expression of the working class and the 'carrier' of its ideology, applied Gramsci's analysis in two ways. First, it has established a presence in all aspects of social life — leisure, culture, youth movements, the factory floor, and so forth. The party is surrounded by an impressive array of ancillary and allied organisations — including large and active women's and youth movements, cultural associations, newspapers and journals, and, not least, the communist-oriented, but not controlled, trade union, the CGIL, the largest in Italy.

Secondly, it has pursued an 'alliance strategy' — an attempt to attract the support of a variety of social groups around the hub of its solid working class base. In the party's view, 'hegemony cannot be exercised without unity of the broadest strata of urban and rural workers, and without a vast system of alliances. These alliances must be based on a convergence of concrete interests, and on the need to find solutions to the big problems — historical and modern — facing Italian society. Hence the policy of alliance between the working class and the peasants, the popular masses of the south, the intellectuals and the working middle classes'.[19]

A necessary corollary of this is that the party's efforts to weld together broad alliances constitutes a long-term, firmly based strategy, and not a series of tactical measures. This fits in with the second of Gramsci's conceptions, which the party claims to apply.

Gramsci distinguished between two ways of seeking power. Using a military metaphor, he termed these the 'war of movement' and the 'war of position'. The first referred to Bolshevik-style insurrection, which he regarded as appropriate for underdeveloped, semi-feudal societies, but not for the sociologically complex and advanced societies of the west. For these societies he recommended a 'war of position' — that is a strategy of slowly, patiently investing the citadels of power in 'civil society' by an energetic pursuit of the contest against the ruling class on the economic, political and cultural fronts. This struggle for ideological supremacy is clearly quite different from social-democratic objectives-building, in the sense of gaining majority support for piecemeal reforms on the basis of the lowest common denominator. 'The point that distinguishes our conception from the traditional theory and practice of social-democratic parties', one senior communist leader commented, 'is not whether we accept or do not accept the concept of gradualism'. Rather it lies in the party's 'vision of advancing towards socialism and building socialism', and its efforts to widen popular participation in all areas of decision-making, in such a way as to change the balance of power between the major social classes.[20]

Thus, both strategies are gradualist in the sense of not contemplating a sudden assault on existing structures of power. The difference resides in the fact that social-democracy, or its dominant right-wing, has been effectively incorporated into bourgeois society, politically and intellectually. Italian-style communism avows a commitment to supersede it. It should be added that the latter bears a much closer resemblance to the pre-1914 classical social democracy of Karl Kaustsky, and the Austro-Marxists than the former. In this sense, it may well be that the PCI has become 'social-democratic'.

Precisely where the historic compromise fits into this wider strategy is a matter for discussion. It seems highly unlikely that in elaborating his theories, Gramsci ever envisaged a communist-Christian Democratic government coalition. More relevantly, it is less than certain that the aims the PCI has set itself can be realised through a political arrangement with the Christian Democratic establishment.

PCI and Soviet Union

Socialists have traditionally been unhappy with the close links that communist parties maintain with Moscow. However, the PCI, unlike the French Communist Party, was never reduced to the status of the obedient servant of the Kremlin. From the 1950s onwards, in particular, the PCI began to assert its independence from Moscow more openly. This process has continued. At the Conference of European Communist Parties, held in East Berlin, in the summer of 1976, Berlinguer made a point of reaffirming the full freedom of his party to determine its own stand on political issues. 'Ours is a free meeting,' the Italian leader declared, 'among autonomous and equal parties, which does not seek to lay down guidelines for or bind any of our parties.' For the benefit of his Soviet listeners, he added: 'There is not and cannot be any leading party or leading state'.[21]

The PCI has also participated in the struggle for human rights and democracy in the eastern bloc. Its efforts have become more pronounced as unrest has mounted in eastern Europe in recent years. The Italian communists have sought to persuade the Polish authorities to act with clemency towards those arrested after the disturbances over price rises in June 1976. They have given support to the Committee for the Defence of Workers, set up to protect imprisoned workers.[22]

Ever since the Prague Spring, and the Soviet invasion of Czechoslovakia, the PCI has taken a keen interest in events in that country. Dubcek's 'socialism with a human face' was warmly supported by the Italian party, and his brutal overthrow did much to widen the rift with Moscow. At the European communist summit, Berlinguer was the only speaker to broach this delicate subject, drawing attention to the PCI's 'critical judgement' of Soviet actions.[23] The PCI has positively responded to appeals from the Charter 77 group of Czech dissidents, and Berlinguer has denounced the behaviour of the Prague regime. Communist parties, he stated, 'do not have the right or duty to insist on obedience, to force people to accept any specific concept of the world, or to limit intellectual freedom in any way whatsoever'.[24]

The PCI's willingness to condemn individual acts of repression has not, so far, been matched by a similar disposition to scrutinise more critically the Soviet system itself. This question raises difficult problems for the PCI leadership, which has responded cautiously and warily.

The party's ambiguous relationship with Moscow creates problems for its political strategy, the historic compromise — discussed in detail later — which aims to attract as broad a range of opinion behind a programme of social and economic reforms. Whilst the party's opponents are always likely to utilise 'red scare' tactics to impede its progress, these efforts are aided by the PCI's continued association with Moscow. What is in question is not whether the PCI intends to impose a Soviet-style regime on Italy — a most unlikely eventuality, as argued above. The source of embarrassment for the party is the common identification — at one time actively promoted by the PCI — between communism, as such, and the Soviet social and political system.

The PCI can repeat indefinitely that the Italian socialism which it aspires to create will be nothing like Soviet and eastern European socialism for a whole series of good historical reasons. It can multiply its demonstrations of independence of the USSR. But doubts will always linger, even among those not ill-disposed towards it, until the PCI meets full square the problem of the nature of the Soviet system.

Though stressing its complete autonomy from Moscow, the PCI has always striven to maintain good relations with the Soviet Union. These would undoubtedly be jeopardised if the party embarked on a full-scale, critical analysis of Soviet society. Given admission that the exercise of fundamental democratic rights is obstructed in the USSR, the party has been reluctant to face the question of why, 60 years after the revolution, this should be so.

In the past, the leadership explained the survival of repressive practices in terms of 'deviations'. More recently, in view of the systematic nature of the lack of democracy, it has become more difficult to sustain the notion of 'anomalies' and 'deviations'. Recognizing this, the party is now prepared to offer a more general explanation: the

USSR has a socialist economic structure, but a non-socialist superstructure. True, an advance on earlier explanations, it is still not wholly convincing — especially for an avowedly Marxist party. For how could a superstructure remain so unaffected by the economic base, over so long a period of time, to allow such a discrepancy? A resolution to this question involves the delicate matter of how meaningful it is to describe the Soviet Union as a socialist society at all.

The party is not unaware of this. Recently, its review, *Rinascita,* stated that the Soviet question is not an intellectual problem, but a political one. This suggests that the leadership does not now, in private, consider the Soviet system socialist — indeed, in view of the Togliattian definition of socialism 'as democracy taken to its extreme limit' adopted by the party, it is difficult to see how it could — but does not deem it expedient to say so publicly.

One can understand the reasons for this reticence. First, it would have to spell out the characteristics of a socialist society, and how and why the Soviet Union does not fulfil them. Second, it would have to define the nature of the Soviet regime, and, more damaging, how and why the party had been unable to recognise earlier that the Soviet Union and eastern European states are not, and never were, socialist. Third, there is the effect on the party's militants' sense of identity — many of them, according to a recent survey, still regard the Soviet Union as a true socialist society. Fourth, the denunciation of the Soviet Union as a bureaucratic regime would encourage questioning of the mechanism of democratic centralism, and hence the leadership's means of controlling the party.

Finally, the very moderation of its domestic policies — described above — combined with its striving for an arrangement with the main party of the right, may, paradoxically, make it more difficult for the PCI to sever its connections with the Soviet Union. Traditional ties of friendship with the 'socialist camp' can be exploited by the leadership to reassure worried activists, disturbed by the historic compromise, that the party remains true to its commitment to fundamental social change. In other words, the Soviet connection becomes a symbol of the PCI's radicalism — whatever the doubts privately entertained by its leaders about Soviet-style 'socialism'. For all these reasons, it is likely that the party will continue its present tactic of disassociating itself from the more unsavoury features of the Soviet system, while seeking to preserve good working relations with the USSR.

Historic Compromise

The strategy of alliances, with its goal of gradual supercession of the existing social system, should not be equated with the historic compromise. The party, still, in its declarations of principle, gives priority to a working class and left unity, which it sees as an essential and irreducible part of its overall strategy. Its *Draft Theses for the 15th National Congress* in spring 1979 declares that 'the policy of unity of the workers' movement constitutes the most valid basis for the necessary political and electoral advance of the left as a whole', and that 'unity between the PSI and the PCI . . . represents one of the linchpins of the PCI's unity-oriented strategy'.[25]

Nevertheless, whilst a left-wing parliamentary majority is regarded as a 'fundamental goal', the party holds that 'such a majority would not in itself be sufficient to guarantee a process of democratic transformation, and transition to socialism'[26]. For this an arrangement with the Christian Democrats (DC) is necessary. The problem here is whether such an arrangement would not subvert the purpose for which it is sought. The historic compromise is described as an agreement of all democratic and progressive forces. To make this credible, the DC needs to be depicted as a 'popular' party. In Berlinguer's words, the DC 'is a party tied to the interests of big economic concentrations of vested interests, and of parasite groups. But it is also a party which, by virtue of its origins, of some of its traditions, and of the presence in it and in its electorate of broad masses of the middle class, peasants, women and workers, must also take account of popular demands and aspirations'.

Unfortunately for the credibility of this analysis, the DC is losing its popular character and is drifting to the right, politically and in terms of the social make-up of its electorate. Its more progressive wing has steadily lost ground, with the younger Christian Democratic MPs tending to be more conservative and anti-communist than their longer-serving colleagues.

There is a yet more serious obstacle to the fulfilment of historic compromise. One of the prime planks in the PCI's programme is the need to combat corruption, waste and political nepotism in the public sector. State-owned corporations like IRI and ENI have long been infested with the disease of 'clientellism' and parasitism — that is, they are part of a vast patronage network, encouraged and sustained by the Christian Democrats.

The communists recognise that if the reforms they advocate are to be implemented, the administrative agencies will have to be overhauled and cleansed of malpractices. 'Of fundamental importance,' the draft theses for the 1979 party congress declare, 'is a reform of the public administration, and, in general, of all the instruments for government of the economy. Without such a reform, all attempts to change the make-up of public spending and improve the capacity for spending for investments and social services will be doomed to failure'.[27]

This judgement would be widely accepted. But could such long-overdue and vital reforms be carried out with the concurrence of the Christian Democrats? The problem is twofold. First, they are the main political expression of finance and industry — and be it said, of many ordinary Catholics — and hence reluctant to envisage sweeping reforms of any type. Second, they are also an old-style party of patronage, which uses the civil service and state industries as employment opportunities for faithful or potential supporters, and ensures the loyalty of the organisation by giving top jobs to reliable party men. Would any agreement with the DC survive a determined communist effort to eradicate the clientelle system and institute a system of promotion by merit, and not by favour? It is hard to see why the

Christian Democrats should co-operate in removing a vital source of support.[28]

Whether the historic compromise is a feasible strategy or not, one thing is clear — it marks a sharp break from the politics of sudden and cataclysmic change. By its nature, it is an affirmation of faith in a gradual route to socialism, paved by a series of reforms. Sceptics may doubt the sincerity or durability of this reformist strategy — just as they often turn a jaundiced eye to the general notion of Eurocommunism. This, however, assumes that alterations in the political direction of a party can be made at will. It also implicitly perceives parties as static organisations, impervious to changes emanating from both within and from society at large. In reality, unless a party insulates itself entirely from its social environment — which the PCI has never done — it will inevitably respond to changes in that environment, some of which, indeed, it may have helped to bring about. In other words, there is a constant interaction between parties and societies, both of which are dynamic rather than static phenomena.

As noted earlier, the PCI always strove to avoid political isolation and indeed, in contrast to the PCF, threw itself into society in order to assert its own hegemony. By inserting itself into all the 'folds and creases' of society — Togliatti's phrase — and, by forging links with a host of variegated social groups, the PCI sought to establish itself as the dominant electoral force in Italian politics. This strategy had certain implications for the character and role of the party, whether intended or not. This can be illustrated by glancing at the part it plays in the area in which it is most solidly implanted, the red belt of central Italy.

In the red belt, communist efforts have been triumphant, with repeated electoral victories at municipal, provincial and regional level. But to be assured of continued support from small traders, artisans, manufacturers and peasants — from whom, in the red belt, it enjoys significant electoral backing — the PCI has to effectively articulate their interests and viewpoints. Hence, instead of being primarily the political expression of the working class, however broadly defined, the PCI now, in its political activity, has come to represent a wider spectrum of social groups. It has to combine the interests of divergent and sometimes contending social groups, in its policy-making structure.

Traditional communist thinking, from Gramsci to Togliatti onwards, has anticipated such a coalition of the under-privileged, under the moral and political leadership of the working class that is, the party. It has long emphasised that the real enemy of the people is 'the monopolies'. The advantage of this is that, notionally at least, the vast majority of the population can be recruited into an 'anti-monopolies' crusade. However, it overlooks the fact that much of the traditional middle class is stubbornly conservative in outlook, and — though they may be attracted by attacks on 'the monopolies' and various fiscal and credit concessions proposed by the PCI — they are hardly likely to support radical social changes.[29]

The danger is that, out of fear of alienating any of these lower-middle class groups it has assiduously courted, the PCI may find its room for manoeuvre restricted. At worst, the effort to woo these groups might erode the dynamism of the party, diminish its ability to devise cogent and radical programmes, and reduce its range of strategic options.[30]

The Compromise Impasse

Western commentators too often imagine a scenario in which the innocent are beguiled by the sirens of Eurocommunism. The danger — as the late Ugo La Malfa, of the Republican Party wrote is . . . 'not that Italy will meet the fate of Czechoslovakia, Poland and Hungary. It is that a government based on co-operation among Christian Democrats, socialists and communists might be just as ineffective as those past governments made up of Christian Democrats and the socialists'.[31] It would be yet another instance of the Italian phenomenon of *transformismo* — the incorporation into the governing elite of radical opposition groups.

So far, the PCI has been spared this fate — partly because the Christian Democrats have refused to allow any communists into the cabinet. Since the summer 1976 elections, Italy has been a country searching for a stable government formula. The old centre-right arrangement — Christian Democrats, Liberals, Republicans and Social Democrats — can no longer muster a majority. The socialists have been very wary about reviving the centre-left formula — the parties mentioned with the PSI substituting for the Liberals — which ruled Italy from the early 1960s to the mid-1970s, largely because they incurred electoral unpopularity without much to show by way of reforms achieved in return. In the last three years, the ingenuity of the Italian political class has been strained to the utmost to devise means by which communist support for Christian Democrats could be secured without, however, actually giving ministerial positions to communists. Until February 1979, the PCI was part of a 'programmatic majority', giving parliamentary support to a minority DC administration, enjoying rights to consultation, but barred from direct participation in the government.

This, in event, meant responsibility without power. The PCI's electoral fortunes began to decline as witnessed by local government elections, and discontent within the party gradually intensified. A major source of the party's dwindling prestige was its increasing identification with unpopular government measures to tackle the country's serious economic difficulties. Italy faces many of the same problems as the UK — high unemployment, inflation, low growth, widening regional disparities, and an unsteady balance of payments — all exacerbated, in Italy's case, by an appallingly inefficient civil service. The Andreotti government sought to cut inflation and revive investment by a policy of wage restraint. Industrialists and bankers hoped that, in exchange for some say in policy formulations, the communists would use their influence with the unions to restrain their wage demands.

They were not to be entirely disappointed. Moving considerably beyond Gramsci's concept of a 'war of position', the PCI adopted extremely cautious views on wages and economic policy. The party's economic spokesman, Giorgio Napolitano, has commented that 'the need to fight inflation and to devote a larger share of resources to investment also implies that the cost of labour must be contained', although, he adds, such a 'policy of austerity . . . must be based on criterion of social justice'.[32]

The trade union rank and file has not responded enthusiastically to such advice, and PCI influence on the shop floor has undoubtedly dwindled. The communist leadership of the largest union federation, the CGIL, has earned a reputation for being 'reasonable'.[33] But the grass roots, both within the CGIL and the PCI, and the Catholic and social democratic unions, have been calling for resistance to the government's deflationary economic policy. The greater freedom of debate now permitted in the PCI has enabled activists to air their grievances.

Despite growing pressure from trade unions and their own rank and file, the PCI leaders encountered mounting resistance from the Christian Democrats to any concessions. One student of the PCI explained the Christian Democratic strategy as 'attempting to maximise the PCI's visible responsibility for government behaviour, while keeping real communist influence at a minimum'. This would gradually lead, they hoped, to the erosion of the communist credibility and support.[34]

This strategy has been bearing fruit — as some communist leaders now admit.[35] The slippage of its electoral backing, indicated by local elections and opinion polls, growing unhappiness at the grass roots, as well as the obduracy of the Christian Democrats, persuaded Berlinguer and his colleagues to return to the opposition, and thus precipitate fresh elections, a year before Parliament's four-year term has elapsed.

The results, for the PCI, were as bad as had been expected. Its voting strength fell back from 34 per cent to 30 per cent of the electorate, and it lost 1½ million votes. The results are given below.

ITALIAN GENERAL ELECTION, JUNE 1979
CHAMBER OF DEPUTIES RESULTS
(1976 results given in brackets)

	Percentage	Seats
Christian Democrats (DC)	38.3(38.7)	262(262)
Communist Party (PCI)	30.4 (34.4)	201(228)
Socialist Party (PSI)	9.8(9.6)	62(57)
Social Movement (fascists) (MSI)	5.3(6.1)	30(35)
Social Democratic Party (PSDI)	3.8(3.4)	20(15)
Radical Party (PR)	3.4(1.1)	18(4)
Republican Party (PRI)	3.0(3.0)	16(14)
Liberal Party (PLI)	1.9(1.3)	9(5)
Far left parties	2.2(1.5)	6(6)
Others	1.3(0.5)	4(3)

It should be noted that the forces of the left — PCI, PSI, Radicals, the far left — suffered only a slight loss of support, from 46.6 per cent in 1976 to 45.8 per cent in 1979. The socialists, who had hoped to pick up a large number of votes, gained only marginally — in contrast to the Radicals, a dynamic civil rights-oriented, new left party, who tripled their percentage of the poll. So communist losses cannot be ascribed to a swing to the right. The left, as a whole, stood its ground. It was the PCI alone which was the object of disaffection.

More important than the actual loss of votes and seats was the psychological blow the party received. Granted, 30.4 per cent was the second best result the party had ever obtained. But the 1979 elections represented the first electoral setback it had suffered since the war. The belief that the rise in popularity of the PCI was inexorable was rudely shattered. In particular, it seems that many young voters turned away from the party as a protest against its policy of accommodation with the Christian Democrats.

Inevitably, the party's poor showing at the polls has led to considerable internal dissension, and renewed questioning of the historic compromise. Yet whereas party leaders, including Berlinguer, have been willing to criticise the way in which it has been implemented, no fundamental re-evaluation of the strategy itself appears likely.

Nevertheless, doubts about the value of seeking a historic compromise will probably continue to grow. The communists have, over the last few years, proved their willingness to compromise — but the Christian Democrats have not. Nor is this surprising. For it is hard to see what they had to gain by a fully-fledged agreement with the PCI.

The PCI proclaims that its long-term intention is to transform society in a socialist direction. It is only natural that big business and its political representatives should display little enthusiasm to aid the party in this project. The DC has no interest in promoting the speedy introduction of communist-sponsored reforms. Indeed, it quite clearly stood to profit by clogging the decision-making process with endless delays. It doubtless calculated that the failure of a government with which the communists were associated would undermine the PCI's public image as an efficient and progressive political force, and disillusion many of its supporters. The slump in communist votes in the 1979 elections is a measure of the shrewdness of this strategy.

All this is part of a wider dilemma. The problem for the PCI, aside from DC reticence, is that however 'moderate' and 'responsible' it might strive to appear, the growth of its power, and of the labour movement as a whole, is likely to frighten the middle classes into intransigent positions. Even if the communists promise to protect their economic interests they are bound to feel that their social status influence and access to governing channels will be reduced. Hence they are likely to continue rallying behind a Christian Democrat party which offers itself as the rock-solid barrier against which the communist tide will break.

Whether, then, the historic compromise, and the consensual road to reform will prove viable, particularly in a period of economic stagnation and intensifying industrial strife, is a question yet to be resolved.

PCI and Socialist Parties: Conclusions

In conclusion, several points can be made. The durability of the PCI's commitment to democratic principles and institutions can no longer be doubted. It accepts a peaceful, parliamentary route to socialism, on the basis of securing as wide a measure of agreement as possible. Its activities in support of human rights and political freedom in the Soviet bloc furnishes further evidence of its adhesion to democratic values.

Of equal interest, the PCI has, in recent years, affirmed its desire for closer collaboration with socialist parties. In a speech to the central committee in October 1975, Berlinguer reasoned that a precondition to the achievement of 'real democratic progress and economic and social renewal in western Europe' is 'a rapprochement and collaboration among the parties that have their base in the working class . . . first and foremost, between the communist and the socialist parties'.[36]

The PCI argues that the growing concentration and internationalisation of capital, and the vulnerability of individual countries, seeking to implement socialist policies, to pressures the international financial and business community can apply, makes greater cooperation between the left and the labour movement across frontiers essential. One of the main barriers to this is the fissure between the communist and non-communist left. This has severely impeded moves towards united action. According to the PCI, however, 'the conditions exist today, through critical dialogues and debate, to open a process that moves towards an overcoming of the historical divergences, and a new unity of the west European workers' movement'. The party — implicitly conceding that at least some responsibility for antagonism between communists and socialists attaches to the former's past attitudes and behaviour — suggests that the shift of west European CPs towards Eurocommunism 'makes the possibility all the more evident'.[37]

In recent years, indeed, contacts between the PCI and various socialist and social democratic parties have multiplied. In 1977, the Labour Party in Britain invited the PCI, with its French and Spanish counterparts, to the party's conference that year. The PCI sent high-level delegations to the conferences of both 1977 and 1978, indicating eagerness to develop closer relations between the two parties. A number of informal meetings have also taken place between Italian communist leaders and members of the Labour Party's national executive committee. In November 1978, the NEC's international sub-committee approved a recommendation encouraging informal discussions with the PCI.

It would be premature to claim historical differences within the west European left have been transcended. But it does appear the positive attitude the PCI is displaying towards socialist parties may help create conditions where old antipathies can gradually be healed, and a new era of fruitful collaboration can open.

FOOTNOTES

1. 'Draft Theses' for the 15th national congress, as printed in *The Italian Communists,* foreign bulletin of the PCI, special issue, 1978, p 9 (henceforth 'Draft Theses').
2. Reprinted in *The Italian Communists,* nos 5-6, September-December 1975, p 49.
3. Reprinted in *The Italian Communists,* no 4, September-December 1975, p 75.
4. Quoted in S. Segre's 'The Communist Question in Italy', in *Foreign Affairs,* vol 54(4), 1976, pp 697, 704.
5. Quoted by Robert D Putnam in 'The Italian Communist Politician' in Blackmer, DLM and Tarrow, S *Communism in France and Italy,* p 187.
6. In a report to the central committee, May 1976.
7. Ugo La Malfa's 'Communism and Democracy in Italy', *Foreign Affairs,* vol 56, no 3, April 1978, p 485.
8. *Ibid.*
9. Robert D Putnam's *The Beliefs of Politicians,* p 185.
10. Putnam in *Blackmer and Tarrow,* p 195.
11. N McInnes's *The Communist Parties of Western Europe,* p 102.
12. P A Allum, *Italy — Republic Without Government,* p 80.
13. A Gramsci's *Prison Notebooks,* p 188-9.
14. G Napolitano's 'The Italian Crisis: A Communist Perspective', *Foreign Affairs,* vol 56, no 4, July 1978, p 799.
15. PCI *Proposta di Progetto a Medio Termine,* July 1977, pp 52-53.
16. 'Draft Theses', p 67.
17. Napolitano *op cit,* p 799.
18. Gramsci *op cit,* p 57.
19. 'Draft Theses', p 13.
20. *The Italian Road to Socialism,* an interview by Eric Hobsbawn with Giorgio Napolitano, 1977.
21. *The Times,* 1 July 1976.
22. *Financial Times,* 21 July 1976.
23. *The Times,* 1 July 1976.
24. *The Guardian,* 20 January 1977.
25. 'Draft Theses', pp 85, 91.
26. *Ibid,* p 91.
27. *Ibid,* pp 67-68.
28. 'The DC has long been identified as the major force promoting the interests of a stratum of small and middle-size entrepreneurs, of a swollen bureaucracy, and a cumbersome public sector.' G. Pasguino's 'Before and After the Italian Elections of 1976', *Government and Opposition,* vol 12 (i), winter 1977. Similarly, a report prepared by Euro-Finance, a research organisation controlled by leading banks in the western world observed, that 'with a following built largely on patronage', the Christian Democrats are 'well aware that, once out of power, the number of CD votes may shrink rapidly'. Quoted in *The Guardian,* 5 Nov 1976. Any attempt to uproot this power of patronage would clearly have the same effect. Incidentally, the same report commented that 'the

Italian communists are by now much closer in spirit to Germany's social democrats than to Soviet communism'.

29   'This lack of discrimination', one writer argued, 'is potentially self-defeating, for various social strata oppose the drift of contemporary capitalism for many reasons, not all of which are progressive — for example, Poujadism in France — and many of which are contradictory'. Essay by Hellman in *Blackmer and Tarrow, op cit*, p 381.

30   One leading student of Italian politics has enquired whether the role of PCI Red Belt mayors as 'shrewd political entrepreneurs', mediating an assemblage of diversified social interests, may not hamper their ability to 'assist in aggressive social or political strategies were the circumstances to warrant it'. Essay by Blackmer in *Blackmer and Tarrow*, p 620.

31   La Malfa, *op cit*, p 488.

32   Napolitano in *Foreign Affairs, op cit*, pp 796, 797.

33   *The Times*, 17 January 1977.

34   S Hollman, 'The Italian CP: Stumbling on the Threshold?', *Problems of Communism*, November-December 1978, p 40.

35   At the recent PCI congress, one leader, Armondo Cassutto, declared that the Christian Democrats had not sought to reach agreement with the communists, but to harm their image among the masses. He added: 'In these situations we have often been slow to recognise their intentions, slow to react with the proper energy, and slow, finally, to sever a relationship which threatened to become one of simple subordination'. *The Guardian*, 4 April 1979.

36   Reprinted in *The Italian Communists*, nos 5-6, Sept-Dec 1975, p 77.

37   'Draft Theses', p 49.

2 FRANCE: EUROCOMMUNISM AMIDST UNCERTAINTY

Of all the major continental communist parties, the most enigmatic is probably the French Communist Party. This is not just because the party's evolution in recent years seems so confused and paradoxical, or because its exact position is obscure — or perhaps badly misunderstood — but because the PCF appears to have inexplicably thrown away the chance of a left victory at the polls in 1978 by quarrelling with the socialists. This long and acrimonious quarrel is discussed below. But it helps to add to the mystery of what exactly the PCF wants, and it serves to reinforce the party's image in some quarters as unreformed Stalinist.

For these reasons, and many others, the French Communist Party is one of the most important Eurocommunist parties. And it is important for observers to be aware of what it represents inside France. Furthermore, the French Communist Party is one of the major political parties of the European left, and it has been so since it first emerged as a national party in the Popular Front of 1936, with 15 per cent of the vote and 72 deputies. However, since that time, the French left has been divided into the PCF and a non-communist component — itself frequently divided and quarrelling — and relations have rarely been good. However, French communism has remained a massive force on the left, which, during the post-war years, only once fell below one-fifth of the vote; and in the late 1940s claimed over a quarter of the votes cast.

Yet French communism has been unable to capitalise on its own strength. Particularly during the cold war years, and even during the Fifth Republic, the PCF was isolated and distrusted as the antidemocratic agent of a foreign power — 'neither of the left or of the right, but of the east' — as the socialist leader, Guy Mollet, once said. French communists, of course, brought this on themselves through their pro-Moscow, Stalinist behaviour, and their series of quasi-insurrectionary strikes in the years 1947-48. The result was, though, that only with the waning of the cold war was it possible for the French left to reunite.

French Communism began to move back into the mainstream of French politics as the 1960s progressed and this could be seen in a number of ways, through the 1962 electoral agreement between socialists and communists with the joint Left Presidential candidate (Mitterrand) in 1965, with the 'common platform' of the Left in 1968 and so on. But despite these electoral and tactical/strategic moves, the question of the Communist Party's true nature has remained. Whatever criterion one adopts — differences with Moscow, acceptance of the European Community or of the Atlantic Alliance, acceptance of pluralism and public debate within the party, integration into the local 'bourgeois' political system, abandonment of references to classic Marxist-Leninist theory, gradualism in economic policy and political strategy — one can say that the French Communist Party (PCF) lags behind its Italian brother on the Eurocommunist road; which is not to prejudge whether or not it will in time advance to the point which PCI has now reached.

Nevertheless, the PCF has evolved more rapidly in the mid-1970s than at any time in its existence. In this sense changes within it have been more sudden and dramatic than in its sister parties in Spain (the PCE) and Italy (the PCI). Yet doubts still linger. Unlike the PCI and PCE, changes within the PCF were not clear cut and where they occurred at all they were late and hedged about with restrictions to the extent that they, at times, seemed hardly credible.

Nevertheless there have been significant shifts within French Communism and these have occurred in more or less the same areas as in the other large CPs of Latin Europe. These are factors identified as 'Eurocommunism' by outside observers (a term which French Communists have only recently accepted) — and they include relations with Moscow, democracy and freedom, party organization and the vexed problem of the Unity of the Left.

All are naturally controversial and there is no consensus about the nature and extent of changes within the PCF. It is the major problem for the French left, and the effect of any changes will have an impact throughout the entire European left and therefore need to be examined more clearly.

The PCF and Moscow

Georges Marchais, French communist General Secretary, recently observed that communist policy was 'made in Paris, not in Moscow'. Unfortunately this is not the first time French communists have made such a statement, and on all previous occasions it has been quite untrue. One of the main features which separated communism from socialism was the strict adherence of the CPs to Moscow, and their willingness to carry out Russian instructions. However, there are solid indications that PCF attitudes to and relations with Moscow have undergone a distinct evolution.

The slow, painful process of PCF emancipation from the Soviet embrace began in the 1960s. In 1966, for the first time, the party criticised Moscow for an act of repression — namely, the imprisonment of two Soviet dissidents, the writers Sinyavsky and Daniel. But the real landmark — as for so many other communist parties — was the Warsaw pact invasion of Czechoslovakia. The PCF reproved the Kremlin for the invasion — but more mildly than the Italian party, and undoubtedly after much heart-searching. With the gesture made, the party's immediate instinct was to try and contain the damage. The post-Dubcek regime of Gustav Husak has always enjoyed better relations with the PCF than with either the PCI or PCE.

Until autumn 1975 the PCF adopted an attitude to the Soviet Union which differed from both the pro-Sovietism of the Portuguese Communist Party and the more independent stance of the PCI and PCE. Specific Soviet Union actions were criticised, but the leadership of the Soviet Party (CPSU) in the world communist movement continued to be accepted. Again, in 1975, the PCF expressed its solidarity with the Portuguese Communist Party — then under attack by the PCI, PCE and the French and Portuguese socialists for seeking to gain power by undemocratic means.

However, in November 1975 the PCF suddenly aligned itself with the PCI. The two parties published a joint statement, which stressed a general 'concordance of solutions' for situations with a 'common character' in highly developed countries. Then, in January 1976, Marchais declared that the PCF would now drop the word 'dictatorship of the proletariat', which no longer accurately expressed its policy. After restating the PCF's attachment to democracy, pluralism of political parties and freedom of speech, he added:

> 'We consider that the principles which we enunciate concerning socialist democracy are of universal value. It is clear that we have a disagreement with the Communist Party of the Soviet Union about this problem.'[1]

This statement is clearly crucial, and may be said to mark the PCF's true ideological breach with Moscow. Until then the 'French road to socialism' had been different from the Soviet one, but leading essentially to the same goal. Now it was proclaimed to embody principles of universal application, which the Soviet Union was condemned for failing to observe.

In January 1976 the arrival in France of Leonid Plyushch — whose internment in a Soviet psychiatric hospital the PCF had earlier denounced — provided the occasion for a further demonstration of hostility to Soviet repression and, for the first time, positive solidarity with its victims. PCF leaders appeared alongside Plyushch at a press conference and associated themselves with his struggle for democracy in the Soviet Union. To reiterate the point, Marchais did not attend the 25th CPSU congress in February that year — a conspicuous absence, as PCF leaders usually attended the Soviet Party congress religiously.

At the PCF's own 22nd congress in 1976, Marchais said: 'We cannot allow the communist ideal, whose object is the happiness of mankind, and on behalf of which we call upon the working people to struggle, to be besmirched by acts which are unjust and unjustified'.[2] But the limits of the change were equally clearly set. Internationally, the Soviet Union remained a socialist state, under which 'great historical progress' had been accomplished, and with which the PCF was still involved in 'the common struggle against imperialism, and for our great common goals'.

Since 1976, the tide of PCF criticism of the Soviet Union has ebbed somewhat. Contacts and exchanges have been stepped up. At the most recent PCF congress, in spring 1979, Marchais described the balance sheet of the Soviet bloc as 'globally positive'. The party continues to regard eastern European countries as 'socialist', and has been reluctant to engage in any searching analyses of their social and political systems.

On the other hand, though socialist-communist tension in France could have paved the way for a PCF rapprochement with the Russians — who never liked the left alliance — relations have not become noticeably more close. For example, the French delegation to the 60th anniversary of the Russian revolution in Moscow was not led by Marchais, but by Paul Laurent, a noted party 'liberal'. Thus whilst the PCF has been more reticent than the PCI, and especially the PCE, in re-evaluating its relations with Moscow, it has also, at long last, cut the umbilical cord which for so long tied it to the Soviet Union. It has now, belatedly, accepted the doctrine of polycentrism, first articulated by the Italian communist leader, Togliatti. L'Humanité, the party's official organ, gave expression to this basic shift in outlook when it said:

> 'For the concept according to which the communist parties were "detachments" of a world movement . . . was substituted the idea of the independence and equality of the various communist parties; the idea that the international communist movement is not, and cannot be a centralised organisation; the conviction that no party or group of parties is in a position to define an exemplary line or strategy which would be valid for others. In solidarity, because they are communists, it is together that the parties constitute the world's communist movements.'[3]

But the journey from 'polycentrism' to a proper and critical re-examination of the character of the Soviet experiment is a long and difficult one. The PCF has, so far, exhibited less willingness to embark on it than either its Spanish or Italian counterparts.

PCF and Democracy

Considerations of the French Communist Party's view of Russia, and of the Soviet system, raises the question of the PCF's view of pluralistic democracy. From the French communists' view of the suppression of human rights in the east, and their condemnation of Russian behaviour on these matters, it might be assumed, naturally enough, that the PCF is an openly and unambiguously democratic party. However, because of CP hesitations over democracy, still apparent unfortunately, and because of the recent history of French communism, things are still obscure.

In 1947 Maurice Thorez, the then French Communist Party leader, gave a famous interview to *The Times*, in which he emphasised that the French road to socialism would be the 'parliamentary road'. However, the impact of this avowal was reduced by the series of quasi-insurrectionary strikes orchestrated by French and Italian communists in autumn 1947. These strikes contributed to the belief, which hardly needed bolstering, that the PCF intended to seize power through a revolutionary coup d'etat. In fact, their significance was primarily international. They were part of a campaign to weaken the west, organised by the Kremlin in pursuit of its foreign policy objectives. The French communists never seem to have seriously considered the forcible seizure of power.

Yet French communism continued to use eastern European language in talking about popular 'democracy', and condoned socialist 'democracy' in the east for many years. Communists were particularly mealy-mouthed about pluralism, or the multi-party system, and claimed, until recently, to see in eastern Europe evidence that they were true multi-party systems. Nevertheless, in the last 15 years precision has been added to this aspect of the PCF view of democracy. The 1968 'Champigny Manifesto', a key PCF document, said that those powers which 'declared for socialism' would play a full part in France with the PCF in power. But what did the PCF see as a 'declaration for socialism'?

For many years the PCF's reply remained unclear on this point, and further communist proclamations did not entirely produce clarification. The question, put another way, of whether the PCF would be willing to relinquish power achieved by parliamentary means, no doubt, remained open. Communists implied that the popular acclamation of any left government would be so great, overwhelming and unanimous that their resignation or ejection would never occur, because it would never be called for. So much was mere evasion — just as the question of how much successive governments could undo the communists' work was never properly tackled, let alone answered. It was because of this kind of theoretical obscurity about democracy and other matters that many socialists remained anxious about the PCF leadership's real intentions.

The key issues for the non-communist left were the acceptance of a multi-party, as against a one-party system, and the willingness of the PCF to surrender power if defeated at the polls. In negotiations over the Common Programme in 1972 the socialists insisted on a specific pledge to relinquish power if defeated in an election, since to omit it would inevitably be taken as admitting an intention to hold on to power by undemocratic means if necessary. The PCF eventually agreed, but insisted on inserting a curiously worded rider. The relevant passage in the common programme reads as follows:

> 'If the country refused its confidence to the majority parties, the latter would surrender power and resume the struggle in opposition. But the chief task of the democratic government, whose existence implies the support of a popular majority, will be the satisfaction of the toiling masses; and the government will therefore be strong in the ever more active confidence that the masses will place in it.'[4]

The PCF therefore affirmed in principle its willingness to accept defeat, while hastening to reassure its supporters that it did not expect the pledge would ever have to be honoured. Similar equivocation appears in Marchais' book *Le Défi Démocratique,* published in 1973. He pledged full support for a multi-party system, but threw into doubt its meaning by instancing the GDR as a multi-party state.

By 1976, the PCF came to recognise that this kind of statement was undermining its credibility. At its 22nd congress the leadership repudiated the 'dictatorship of the proletariat', and avowed its full support for the parliamentary road to socialism and political pluralism. Yet characteristically, the decision to drop the 'dictatorship of the proletariat' was taken without any consultation with ordinary party members.

Despite French communist evolution on the issues of democracy, party pluralism, and the party's abandonment of the notion of the 'dictatorship of the proletariat', it remains distrusted — partly because of the ambiguity of its formulations, but, more importantly, because of its failure to apply the democratic principles it professes to its own internal workings.

PCF Party Structure

Abandonment of the notion of the 'dictatorship of the proletariat' was a sound tactical move, removing one of the most inconvenient expressions from the communist vocabulary, and enabling the PCF to emphasise its new attachment to democracy and liberty.

But neither democracy nor liberty are particularly evident in the structure of the party itself. Internally, communist party organisation is quite undemocratic and, despite post-1978 election discontent from Parisian and intellectual quarters, the leadership control over the hierarchy has remained complete, as far as can be ascertained. French communists continue, therefore, to be composed of handpicked nominees, and to vote leadership propositions unanimously. However, in order to place the French communist party's view of itself and the importance of the party organisation in perspective, it is necessary to describe the PCF's Leninism, and to say why it is particularly important in France.

Lenin's contribution to Marxism, and where the Bolshevik party definitely departed from the social-democratic tradition, was twofold — first the assertion that proletarian interests were identical with those of the communist party, and, second, his vision of the communist party as a highly organised group of professional revolutionaries who provided leadership and guidance to the proletariat. Lenin commented about workers' movements that 'history has shown that the working class, exclusively, and by its own efforts, is able to develop trade union consciousness'.[5] He then distinguished between the 'vanguard' or 'guiding nucleus' of the mass movement on the one hand, and the social democrats and trade unions on the other. This vanguard party was the vehicle of revolution, and, according to Lenin, incarnated the objective interests of the working class. Trotsky, later echoed by Rosa Luxemburg, wrote: 'Lenin's methods lead to this — the party organisation at first substitutes itself for the party as a whole, then the central committee substitutes itself for the party organisation, and finally a single man substitutes himself for the central committee'.[6] After the Russian revolution, the party and the state fused, and Stalin emerged as dictator over them both. So the leading role of the party became a substitute for the historic role of the proletariat in Lenin's thought, and in communist practice. Hence the way for Stalinism was prepared. It is, therefore, the 'vanguard' role of the party — not the 'dictatorship of the proletariat' — which is the quintessence of communist organisation and communist uniqueness. And for French communists, the party is still seen as the leader, organiser, and educator of the masses. It retains, in other words, in theory and in practice, the original features which Lenin gave it.

Discipline, centralism and the responsive chain of command moving from the top to the bottom, as introduced by Lenin, remain features of communist organisation in France — as does the pyramidal structure of cells based on residence and workplace. It is pertinent to point out here that this is not true of the 'non-Bolshevik' Spanish Communist Party, where the old structure has broken down, and which is therefore no more Leninist than the SPD, or British Labour Party. In theory, the cell is still the basic unit of the PCI — though not the PCE, whose members, since 1960 or thereabouts, have not been required to join cells.[7] But in Italy discussion is fairly free, and it appears that in the south Communists are really active only at election time.

Yet the organisational obsession of the French communists has not changed. The bureaucratic structure of the French party is still enormously important. Policy is still revealed, not discussed or adjusted. And this was true even of the PCF's liberalising 12th congress. The workplace cell, in particular — the institution Lenin intended to distinguish communists from socialists — marks the PCF from other Eurocommunist parties. Attempts to recruit for the PCF have not noticeably changed this feature, and communist recruitment drives, it must be emphasised, do not necessarily break down the organisational structure. The figure of 80,000 given by the PCF as the number of cells in 1978 is inflated, because the recruitment campaign happened in December, when many party cards had practically expired, but not quite. It included 'dormant' members, who might not rejoin. Within this membership, however, two separate elements must be distinguished — the 'nucleus' and the 'transitory'. The transitory were the many who pass through the PCF without remaining for any significant time. The communist party has a high turnover in membership, and has always been a 'parti passoire'. These new people, of course, are not much marked by the old problems of Stalinism and loyalty to the USSR, but they are an unstable group. However, concealed within this vast membership there is the stable nucleus — perhaps a quarter of the party — composed of older militants, in age and the date when they joined, who are much more attached to the party's older ideas. It is this group — much more difficult to observe — which may well determine the party's evolution.

Insofar as the PCF continues to be wedded to a democratic, centralist form of organisation, and the elitist notion of a 'vanguard party', in effect controlled by the party bureaucracy, doubts inevitably linger about the genuineness of the PCF's commitment to political pluralism. The leaders responsible for the PCF's new, more liberal stance are necessarily people who worked their way up through its apparatus during the preceding period. They were people who had accepted the conformism, the tight ideological discipline, and the close identification of the party with the Soviet Union which characterised the party in the 'fifties and early 'sixties. It may be assumed that their motives for imposing a change of style were essentially tactical. It may be argued, though, that no party can integrate itself into a pluralist society without its own character being affected. Further, the PCF's constant emphasis, in recent years, on its attachment to democratic norms and practices is likely to encourage its own members to develop a positive attitude towards them. In addition, it should be borne in mind that most French communists have joined within the last few years, and have been attracted to the party since it adopted its democratic and 'open' image. It may therefore be supposed that, even internally, the party leadership cannot act in a way completely inconsistent with this image, without provoking a grave internal crisis, and the departure of many party members. The transformation undertaken in the last 10 years might not be easily reversible, and the longer the party's present image is maintained, the truer that will be, as militants of the new generation rise to higher positions in its structure.

However, caution is needed here. As already noted, the stable core of members is likely to feel more sympathy for the older, harsher ideas and attitudes with which the party was associated a decade or more ago. Above all, the maintenance of democratic centralism fixes definite limits to PCF liberalism. This form of organisation ensures that candidates for official positions have to be approved by the party hierarchy, and are therefore primarily accountable to the leadership, rather than those they are supposed to represent — hence severely restricting democratic control of the party.

Undoubtedly, the rank and file of the party are now encouraged to discuss general political problems to a much greater extent than used to be the case. But decisions, once taken by the appropriate party organ, are still not supposed to be questioned. Discussion at the party's base takes place within the framework of the cell — a group of 20 people. The cells do not normally communicate directly with each other, but with the section to which they belong — the sections with the federation, and the federations with the central committee. A democratically organised opposition to the leadership or the prevailing line within the party, remains something unthinkable. The leadership, in recent years, has continued to decide and announce important policy changes, with little or no public discussion. One example was the decision to abandon the concept of the dictatorship of the proletariat, announced by Marchais in a radio interview, and voted by a unanimous party congress a month later. Another was the decision to support continued development of France's nuclear strike force, taken by the central committee in May 1977, virtually without debate.

Doubts about the PCF, which have tended to fix on internal organisation questions, were greatly intensified by the party's sudden and unexpected change of course in 1977. It then unleashed a mass of hostile propaganda against its supposed ally — soon to become a partner in government, it was hoped — the Socialist Party.

Union of the Left

The break-up of the union of the left was unexpected — not only because it effectively torpedoed the left's election prospects in March 1978, but also because it represented a sharp shift in communist strategy.

Throughout the 1960s, the PCF had sought to escape from its ghetto by establishing better relations with other left forces. In 1965, it backed Francois Mitterrand in his bid for the presidency. Two years later, it reached an arrangement with the Federation of the Left, an alliance of Socialists and Radicals. This arrangement, and the federation, disintegrated under the impact of the 'events' of May 1968, and relations between the PCF and the non-communist left deteriorated. But, by 1971, the climate had altered again. Mitterrand had re-emerged as undisputed leader of the rejuvenated Socialist Party, committed to a strategy of communist-socialist co-operation. By the following year, the two parties, together with the left Radicals, had jointly signed the 'Common Programme of Government', setting out in some detail the policies a left government would implement if elected to office.

The union of the left, despite intermittent friction between its partners, survived until September 1977, when an acrimonious dispute erupted over updating the Common Programme. The communists and socialists, to the surprise of many observers, failed to resolve their differences in time for the elections. Defeat at the polls was the price they paid. Recriminations over responsibility for defeat inevitably followed and, to date, relations between the erstwhile partners remain rancorous.

Whilst few would absolve the socialists totally from responsibility for the collapse of the union, many attach most blame to the PCF, who, from September 1977, launched a bitter propaganda campaign against its ally. Yet, though the vehemence of the communists' attack was unexpected, their growing discomfort with the results of the alliance with the socialists, so far, was more explicable.

When the PCF threw its support behind Mitterrand's candidature in 1965, the two sections of the left entered a period of co-operation which, despite frequent tension and setbacks, lasted 12 years. All the same, there were fundamental contradictions implicit within the relationships, which were never resolved. It is clear that both embarked on collaboration with different aims and expectations. Whatever the PCF wanted, it was surely not to help Mitterrand build a new and stronger socialist party that could effectively challenge the PCF's predominance on the left, and its leadership of the working class. The PCF leaders, no doubt, understood that this was Mitterrand's intention, for he made it no secret. But they probably calculated that his chances of succeeding were not good. It was reasonable to expect that within a united left the PCF would remain easily the strongest force, and the other parties would serve essentially as channels for attracting voters to an alliance in which the PCF would set the tone.

The communist leadership, throughout the period of co-operation, blew alternately hot and cold, depending on the contingencies of the moment. Sometimes old-style militants had to be reassured. At other stages the need for left-wing unity received greater emphasis. However, two constant concerns were always evident. First, efforts to reach understanding with other left parties had to be combined with ever-greater efforts to strengthen the party itself. Second, there was the need for the left to present itself to the country as not merely united by sentiment, or by tactical self-interest, but also by a programme of concrete policies which could not be dropped. So the central role of the Common Programme could be seen as a source of binding commitment on a future left-wing government, in communist thinking.

Scepticism about the union first seemed to have agitated the PCF leadership in 1974, when a string of socialist successes in by-elections, together with its high standing in the polls, indicated that the PS was emerging as the largest force on the left. Communist leaders were also unhappy the same year about the entry of elements into the Socialist Party, led by Michael Rocard, from the far-left Unified Socialist Party (PSU), regarded as ill-disposed to the PCF. These doubts gradually mounted until they burst into the open in September 1977, over negotiations on updating the Common Programme.

With hindsight, developments within the PS can be seen as bound to cause anxiety within the PCF leadership. The PS, in opinion polls and by-elections, had overtaken the communists as the largest left party, and the gap was widening. Partly as a result of this, Mitterrand and other leading socialists were now treating the PCF in a less than respectful manner.

They concentrated on the task of appealing to floating voters, doubtless assuming the PCF was by now committed to the union of the left beyond recall, and without alternative. They tended to stress that the communists now represented the junior partner in the alliance, with no chance of dominating a future left-wing government. Seeing themselves close to power and responsibility, some PS economic specialists sought to reassure businessmen. A reformist gloss was put on the Common Programme, and a note of 'realism' injected into the left's short-term economic proposals — though concessions to classical 'bourgeois' economics did not go as far as those of the Italian communists.

The main question on which negotiations over the Common Programme finally broke down was the extent of nationalisation. Two aspects of the nationalisation programme aroused heated dispute. The first was whether subsidiaries of firms listed for nationalisation in the Common Programme text should be included with their parent companies. The second was whether a government of the left would propose nationalising any particular company if most of its workforce wanted it to be taken into the public sector.

In the debate between representatives of the three parties — PCF, PS and left Radicals — and in the later debate at public meetings and in the press, other issues were to be added. They included the question of whether compensation was to be paid for nationalising companies specified in the Common Programme, and the overall cost of the programme itself in economic terms.

On related questions of whether subsidiaries of firms listed for nationalisation would be included in extending public ownership, the nature of compensation, and the programme's overall cost it is possible to give the PCF a good deal of benefit in the overall doubt. It is not at all clear how meaningful an extension of the public sector would have been if subsidiaries of specific companies had been ignored. Most big businesses are themselves composed of subsidiaries in the first place. Where would the line lie — in that they did not carry the name of the parent company, in any subsidiary whatever, or what? Without much doubt, Georges Marchais and the PCF leadership might have considered the raising of the question itself brought into question Socialist Party commitment to a major change in the balance of power through ownership.

But it rapidly became apparent that the PCF was not particularly interested in reaching a compromise. The PS was exposed to a barrage of criticism, claiming that it had 'veered to the right', and was secretly preparing a deal with Giscard for a new centre-left government which would exclude the PCF and maintain the economic and social status quo. The Socialists replied by protesting their fidelity to the 1972 programme — even without updating if necessary — and their determination to enter government only as part of the union of the left, rejecting any reversion to the 'third force' strategy.

It is clear the decision to attack the Socialist Party was taken by the top leadership, without consultation with a bewildered rank and file. A number of explanations have been advanced for the PCF's volte-face. Some have discerned the hand of a Soviet leadership fearful of the disturbance to the status quo in Europe a left-wing victory might bring. No strong evidence exists, however, for Soviet involvement. It seems far more probable the communist tactical and strategic change was dictated by domestic considerations.

The strategy of the union of the left had been predicated on the PCF's ability to remain the dominant left force, and the uncontested 'party of the working class'. A left-wing government, in which the PCF would be reduced to the role of junior partner, was of little interest. The inherent risks were too great: the economic circumstances of world depression and the constitutional circumstances of a parliamentary election, leaving the right in control of the all-important Presidency of the Republic were both unfavourable to the left in 1978. A predominantly socialist government would be likely either to collapse quickly, or to pursue an essentially reformist policy, rapidly resorting to classic deflationary measures to stabilise the economy. The examples of Britain and Portugal were often cited.

For many PCF leaders, the root of the problem was not so much what the Socialist Party would *do* — nobody could doubt it had moved the the left since the 1960s, when greater co-operation between communists and socialists was first espoused by the PCF — but what it had *become*. It was the largest party on the left and one which was gaining as much support from the working class as its self-appointed champion, the communists.

As long as gains the PS was making were confined to groups other than the manual working class, the PCF leadership was not too worried. The PS was, after all, performing its 'correct' function of rallying other exploited social strata behind the working class vanguard. But the working class vanguard — and on this point the PCF was quite insistent — was constituted by the Communist Party. In the party's own words, as 'the party of the working class, it is, in effect, the bearer of the interests of all the labouring masses, and of the interests of the nation itself'.[8] The growing PS ability to woo working class votes away from the PCF threatened a fundamental principle of communist orthodoxy — that the party 'objectively' represented all manual workers, and was *the* working class party. This class — for which read the Communist Party — is the class with the historic mission of opening and guiding the way to socialism, though it is destined to be supported by other exploited strata. The PCF is uncompromising on this point.

Much of this antique Leninism is at the basis of quarrels in the French left. Faced with the renovated Socialist Party, the problem of the PCF's identity is at the centre of its current activities — especially with the questioning of key notions. This explains the return to sources, emphasis on organisation, the working class, and the party's 'historic role'. It also pinpoints the decision to reassert the PCF image as the working class party, the poor and the underprivileged, in contrast with a reformist and opportunistic Socialist Party.

The March 1978 elections, though a severe shock for the left, could be interpreted as meeting some of the PCF objectives. The PCF's own share of the vote did decline by comparison with 1973, but not dramatically — from 21.4 to 20.6 per cent. The PS did overtake the PCF for the first time in a national election since 1936, but much less dramatically than it had hoped. Instead of the 27 or 30 per cent predicted by opinion polls, it obtained 22.6 — 24.7, if the MRG votes are included. And the left did not win the election. The perils of governing in unfavourable circumstances were thus escaped.

Conclusion

Eurocommunism, in so far as it can be said to exist at all, means a number of things and a number of changes, all of which tend to a liberalisation in communism. Whether or not such de-Stalinisation and de-bolshevisation is true of other western CPs, the position for the French party is extremely complicated. French communism has not got a 100 per cent record in support of democracy and human rights, and its pronouncements on these issues are watched with close attention. Yet here, and in the other vital area of the relationship with Moscow, the PCF gives cause for concern. It has liberalised and democratised, but qualifications, subsidiary clauses, hedging, and so on, can only serve to increase suspicion of the party's intention. Nevertheless, as argued here, it is probably true to say that the PCF is not a Russian puppet. It does attach great importance to human rights, it does condemn eastern regimes, and it does believe in open, multi-party democracy.

There is still another reason why the PCF is not a completely democratic party — its internal organisation. In the run-up to the PCF's 13th congress in May 1979, internal opposition was treated in typical Stalinist fashion, though perhaps with slightly less heavy-handed lack of subtlety than in the past. Dissidents were denied access to the party press, party organisation was mobilised to support the leadership, factional activity was condemned, and there were a few expulsions from cells for anti-leadership agitation. Liberal intellectuals were isolated and deprived of the means of making their views heard, and the party machine continued on its classically closed, autocratic, hierarchical course. No changes have been made in the PCF's undemocratic structure, and the French communists retain their 'democratic centralist' methods.

Finally, what is the possibility of change in the PCF? This is the question that French socialists have to face, but which is at present difficult to answer clearly. Within the French left, the Communist Party has retained its hold over a working class and differentiated electorate, amounting to some 20 per cent of the vote. It, however, has been unable to advance, and for decades has been incapable of breaking new ground. It is the French Socialist Party which now makes the running in new ideas and in electoral expansion. French communism faces a competitor on the left for the first time since the war.

Whereas in the mid-1960s the French Communist Party faced a weak and divided socialist left, the PCF now has to contend with a dynamic and radical force, which is a serious competitor, and which threatens to reduce the PCF to a mere supporting role to the Parti Socialiste. The absence of a socialist competitor to the PCF in the 1960s allowed it the luxury of a slow, grudging de-Stalinisation, and, unlike the PCI, it has only recently liberalised. The paradox is that had it changed rapidly and efficiently — *Italianised* — in the mid-1960s, before there was a serious socialist challenge, it might well have been able to capitalise on the lack of a socialist party and, like the PCI, have captured a third or more of the electorate. But this never happened, and now the ground which it might have aspired to occupy has been taken by the Socialist Party, which is not predisposed to relinquish it.

Moreover, the PCF is now forced by the Socialist Party to make changes — but it cannot conquer Socialist Party ground by doing so. Even when French socialism was at its most divided and weakest, in 1969, the PCF only managed 21 per cent of the vote, and this seems to be its upper limit. In current conditions, the more the PCF 'liberalises', and the more people lose their fear of communism, the more it becomes possible for the French electorate to vote for the most attractive component of the left, the French Socialist Party.

FOOTNOTES

1. *L'Humanite,* 15 January 1976.
2. *L'Humanite,* 5 February 1976.
3. *L'Humanite,* 30 June 1977.
4. *Le Programme Commun de Gouvernment*, p 10.
5. Lenin's *What is to Be Done?*
6. Quoted in E H Carr's *1917: Before and After,* p 143.
7. Neil McInnes' *Communist Parties in Western Europe*, London, 1975, p 103.
8. Champigny manifesto.

3 SPAIN: EUROCOMMUNISM AND SOCIALISM

In the context of restored parliamentary democracy in Spain, there would seem to be possibilities for a left-wing alliance between the Spanish Communist Party and the Socialist Workers' Party, since there are important similarities in their strategy and programme. But because of this similarity, there is strong competition between them. The Communist Party presents a considerable challenge to the socialists, in trying to occupy socialist political space. The socialists in response, may take one of three possible courses: move to the right; present a hostile rejoinder to Eurocommunism — stressing its inconsistencies, or the undemocratic residues in communist parties; or move towards political convergence — in which case the relative strengths of the two parties, the effects of convergence on their electoral and active support, and the similarities of the programmes are all relevant considerations. The confusion that exists within both socialist and communist parties on these issues was dramatically illustrated in the collapse of the union of the left in France between September 1977 and its electoral defeat in March 1978 — a process discussed elsewhere.

It will be argued here that though the emergence of Eurocommunism should lead to a greater *theoretical unity* of the parliamentary left on programmes of change, it seems likely that *political competition* will increase in the foreseeable future. It will happen where each party is strong enough — either electorally or through trade union support — to try to attain a predominant position in the democratic socialist sphere.

The Political Background

The last parliamentary elections before the 36-years-old dictatorship were held in February 1936, and produced the Popular Front victory. In these elections, the PSOE — Spanish Socialist Workers' Party — won 18.6 per cent of the seats. The PSOE, founded in 1879, was the traditional party of the working class. It presented itself as a class-based radical socialist party, which believed in pluralist democracy and parliamentary politics, while also defending working class extra-parliamentary struggle. The party was divided into a reformist wing, which came to be represented by Prieto, and a revolutionary wing, headed by Largo Caballero under the Second Republic. The typical disharmony of classic Marxist social democracy, between revolutionary objectives and moderate practices, was an important characteristic of the party. Under the Second Republic (1931-1939), the PSOE had an important electoral strength, and the support of a powerful socialist trade union, the UGT, the General Workers' Union, founded in 1888. The PSOE was also an important agency of political socialism, with its *Casa del Pueblo* providing instruments like political education and library facilities at local level.

The PCE, the Spanish Communist Party, was, on the contrary, a small party until the civil war broke out in 1936. In the February 1936 parliamentary elections the Communist Party was a junior partner in the Popular Front, obtaining only 2.96 per cent of the seats. The PCE, founded in 1920 by a section of Socialist Youth, later absorbed a small fraction of the PSOE, which had split in 1921 after leaving the Third International, which it had joined in June 1920.

There were three stages in CP politics under the Second Republic. From April 1931 to August 1932 the party opposed 'bourgeois' radical parties and 'social fascism', in accordance with Comintern strategy. It did not support the new republic. In the second phase, starting in August 1932, the communists supported the republic. The third era, that of the Popular Front, lasted for the rest of the republican period, from summer 1934 to spring 1939. As an example of the new fraternity on the left, the PCE worked with the PSOE and the UGT in an unsuccessful attempt to produce a revolutionary strike in October 1934, and the small communist trade union, CGTU, joined UGT in November 1934.

There were two notable communist party strategies in this period — these concerned alliances and its moderation. Support for the republic and friendly relations with the PSOE had a dual objective. The CP certainly sought to protect democracy and strengthen the left, but, at the same time, wanted to woo to the PCE socialist activists and supporters. The PCE tried gradually to gain control of the UGT. In April 1936, the Communist Youth, led by Carrillo, fused with the Socialist Youth, led by Claudin, to form the Unified Socialist Youth, which became the tool of the PCE. In July 1936 socialists and communists in Catalonia formed a unified party, the PSUC — Unified Socialist Party of Catalonia — which again became a PCE appendage.

This erosion of the allied parties' membership became clearer after the civil war began, when USSR help for the republican government provided the PCE with a strong asset. Communist influence increased substantially after 1936. Its control over Soviet supplies gave the party immense power over the Largo Caballero and Negrin governments. The party had overwhelming influence over the International Brigades for two years from November 1936. The republican' army's political commissars were mostly PCE militants, and the party carried out massive recruitment within the army. The PCE's policy of alliances from 1934 to 1939 was undoubtedly geared towards achieving communist hegemony on the left.

The policy of moderation was also particularly clear during the war. It was seen as necessary for political and military efficiency — since the PCE priority was winning the war. It was also regarded as necessary to maintain the image of a liberal republic, preserving legality — an image needed for western support. PCE political moderation preceded the war, but it became more systematic after its outbreak.

The PCE's moderate policies had several important consequences. Together with the influence of Stalinism, they led to the persecution of the anarchist union, CNT and the far-left party, POUM. They also brought opposition to Largo Caballero, the left-wing socialist President, from December 1936 to May 1937. The Largo Caballero government fell after refusing to dissolve the POUM. The PCE then supported the moderate socialist, Negrin, and, after May 1937, the reversal of anarchist and left socialist collectivisation programmes. The PCE also provoked the end of Largo Caballero's UGT leadership, and contributed to the crisis which lasted from October 1937 to January 1938.

The PSOE also suffered from internal contradictions between 1936 and 1939. While from 1931 to 1933 socialist policies were essentially moderate, the party turned to the left in 1934. It played an important, and again contradictory role in the 1934 revolutionary attempt. But the conflict persisted. The choice was between the defence of the Republic, argued by Prieto, and the revolutionary process, argued by Largo Caballero. Added to this conflict was the dilemma of choosing between support from the USSR or from the capitalist democracies.

The disastrous end of the war in 1939 had two results for the Spanish left. First, the PSOE was almost destroyed as a party. Its huge membership and loose organisation made it — like the anarchist CNT — vulnerable to repression. The bitter struggle with the communist party during the civil war made it increasingly anti-communist. The PSOE moved towards social democracy and control of the party passed into the hands of the right-wing — first Prieto, and later Llopis. In 1943, socialists and republicans set up a Spanish Liberation Front in opposition to the communist-controlled National Union. The socialist leadership in exile then made a grave political miscalculation. It placed its hopes on allied intervention in Spain, on western help in the struggle against Francoism, and on the inability of the Spanish regime to survive the hostile context of post-Francoist Europe.

These hopes proved wrong. From 1951, Franco's survival was assured, but the exiled socialist leadership had meanwhile neglected party organisation and the underground struggle in Spain. The leaders retreated into a defensive position, trying to safeguard an embryonic organisation in exile in the hope of better times.

Socialists however, were active within Spain. They started to organise inside prisons, and in 1944 and 1945 militant socialist groups were amnestied and started to rebuild the party underground. The general underground struggle against the regime increased from 1945 to 1948. There was an attempted general strike in 1947, and the socialist guerrillas survived until 1948. Despite lack of support from the exiled leadership and liberal democracies, the socialist fight in the interior was important throughout the 1950s. Waves of strikes were organised in 1951, 1953 and 1956. Socialist groups were especially active in the working class centres of the Basque country and Asturias.

Socialists suffered heavy repression between 1939 and 1960. After the 1951 strike, UGT militants were shot, and in 1953 the UGT general secretary died from torture. But the socialists lacked strategy and were remote from Spain's internal developments. Repeated efforts by the exiled leadership to control interior groups in, for example, the congresses of 1952 and 1958 led to a serious PSOE crisis which lasted throughout the 1960s.

The second consequence after the war ended was that the PCE became totally dependent on the CPSU. This increased when Dolores Ibarruri, La Pasionaria, was elected general secretary in 1942. The party was strongly Stalinist, both in its internal organisation and relations with other parties. The PCE tried to undermine all other left groups and to absorb their militants.

From 1939 to 1945 the communist party strove to reorganise in secret cells and prisons. It was also involved in guerrilla resistance. From 1945 to 1950 the party leadership moved to Paris and Toulouse, and this period provided three important developments. First, the end of the second world war enabled many Spanish communists in France to rejoin the PCE, and this, coupled with the release of imprisoned militants, increased the number of party cadres. Secondly, the PCE confirmed its support for the legality of the Second Republic and the Republican Government, and tried to make alliances with republicans and socialists. Third, after a meeting with Stalin in 1948, the party agreed to abandon guerrilla actions, which were now hopeless, in favour of a strategy of infiltrating legal institutions, particularly the state-controlled trade unions, of underground struggle to mobilise the working class, and of democratic platforms linked with other groups.

This change in PCE strategy developed throughout the 1950s. The party stressed the need for a democratic front against Francoism, and the strategy of 'national reconciliation' became official in the central committee's declaration in June 1956. In the 1957 official trade union elections, many secret communist party candidates were elected. The PCE tried to work towards cumulative show-downs with the regime — such as the 'day of national reconciliation', 5 May 1958, and the 'general political strike' on 18 June 1959, but all these ventures failed.

The PCE's political assessment was that the country was economically backward, ruled by a superimposed fascist clique, and on the point of economic collapse. The party's 1960 programme tried to attract the middle classes and peasantry — the 'natural allies' — to join the last push against the regime. The 1960s marked PCE supremacy within the left. The PSOE was suffering from its remote leadership in exile, and the PCE reaped the fruits of its infiltration plan as soon as the working class movement re-emerged. Economic growth, the introduction of plant bargaining, and the gradual crisis of the corporatist institutions of working class regimentation were essential factors in this re-emergence.[1] PCE support for Workers' Commissions' movement gave the party an important role in the working class movement. The party gained almost complete control of the Commissions, which eventually became a trade union organisation. At the same time, PCE activity in the student movement gave it a strong influence on student politics. The PCE therefore benefited from their presence with dedicated activists when the working class and student movements gathered momentum.

The communist party influence on both movements enabled it to overcome several important splits in the 1960s. There was a Maoist split in 1963 which led to the PCE-ML, and a Stalinist breakaway in 1969 which eventually became the PTE, the Workers' Party of Spain.

These two rifts were largely due to the PCE strategy of the democratic road to socialism, and broad alliances. But another incident, the expulsion of Fernando Claudin in 1964, reflected the PCE's contradictory conception of democracy. Claudin, Communist Youth general secretary in 1936, was appointed to the political bureau, which later became the executive committee, in 1954. He was expelled, with two other prominent leaders, Semprun and Vicens, because of his critique of the PCE view that Spain was underdeveloped, had a lapsed, bourgeois-capitalist revolution, and dominated by a small clique. This conception ignored the country's capitalist development, since the mid-50s and brought over-optimistic appraisal of the possibilities of change and for democratic fronts. The incident also raised the issue of the PCE's internal authoritarianism and of 'democratic centralism'.

Paradoxically, the PCE assumed most of the Claudin-Semprun theses after expelling them from the party. This was a telling characteristic of PCE politics. It was able to overcome its contradictions through sheer pragmatism, and, because of its firm roots in militant sectors of the working class and student movements. From 1965, the PCE was the dominant force in the illegal student union, the SDE, the Democratic Students Union, and it also controlled the Workers' Commissions (CCOO). From that date, too, its programme moved gradually in the direction of Eurocommunism. First, the party embraced political pluralism — not only in the struggle against Francoism, but in the transition towards socialism and the building of a socialist society. Second, the party adopted a gradualist strategy — and the main factor in advancing towards socialism was considered to be 'the development of productive forces'. Finally, it was accepted that a substantial private sector of small and medium enterprises would be maintained under socialism. From 1965, too, the relationship with the USSR and the CPSU became increasingly problematic. In October 1964 the party paper, *Mundo Obrero*, praised the dismissed Khrushchev. The PCE supported Dubcek all the way, and condemned the Soviet invasion of Czechoslovakia.

The PCE gradually became more autonomous and consolidated its conception of a 'democratic road to socialism'. This was expressed in several publications by Santiago Carrillo, the party's general secretary since 1960. It became incorporated in official party documents during the 1970s, culminating in the party's electoral programme, approved by the central committee in April 1977.

The main traits of the Eurocommunist conception are that a plurality of roads to socialism are accepted, and that in advanced capitalist societies the road must be 'democratic'. Socialism is conceived as a process consisting of a progressive 'extension' of democracy and a strategy of cumulative reforms. This means the concept of the 'dictatorship of the proletariat' cannot be accepted in Lenin's political sense and the Eurocommunist conception of the construction of socialism and of a socialist society has to be different from the Soviet model. The main question here is to what extent does Eurocommunism differ from democratic socialism, and whether it represents a significant advance in relation to the latter's difficulties. The difficulties, in particular, are producing a programme of cumulative reform, resulting in an eventual 'qualitative' change in society, and making egalitarianism compatible with pluralism.

The view the socialists took of Eurocommunism was that the PCE was trying to occupy socialist space and push the PSOE towards social democracy. Socialists stressed the continuities between Eurocommunism and the PCE's historical background. There was nothing new, in their eyes, in either the strategy of alliances or the moderate politics. Eurocommunism was seen as another example of the PCE's considerable ideological opportunism, but needing skilful bending of dogma to adjust it to the exigencies of reality. Through ideological and rhetorical juggling, PCE strategy would always appear either 'revolutionary' or 'responsible', while a similar strategy adopted by other left parties, in apparently similar circumstances, would be presented either as 'adventurist' and 'irresponsible', or as 'collaborationist'.

Socialism and Communism: a Zero-Sum Game?

The PCE believed there was a socialist space to be occupied resulting from the PSOE crisis of the 1960s. A generalised feeling prevailed at the beginning of the 1970s that a strong renaissance of socialism was unlikely. The PSOE seemed weak as an organisation, and the strength of socialism as a movement was largely unknown in the opaque and poorly-informed political world of Francoism. There was a tendency to underestimate the persistence of socialist activism — particularly in Asturias and the Basque Country.

There was, though, a socialist revival after the turn of the decade, which came from a change in the balance of forces within the PSOE, between the exiled groups and those inside the country. Exiled leaders were out of touch with the Spanish political situation, and the interior groups were able to start gaining control of the apparatus. In 1970 the PSOE's 11th congress marked the change. Groups of the interior managed to win nine posts on the new executive committee, but the exiles only seven. Two years later, following the 12th congress in Toulouse, the leadership moved to the interior. This had two effects. The party became more radical, as it was no longer under control of a bureaucracy still influenced by anti-communism. And membership swelled — the socialist movement could now rally round an organisation. At the 13th congress in Suresnes, just outside Paris, in 1974, Felipe Gonzalez was elected general secretary of the party.

The socialist trade union, UGT, was also led from the interior after 1970, and was rapidly recovering strength, expanding beyond its traditional enclaves in the Basque Country — especially the steel and metal industry of Viscaya — and Asturias, particularly in the mines. The re-emergence of the Socialist Party was based on a few thousand members who recruited new militants and acted as informal political representatives of socialism — clandestinely under Francoism's political repression, openly after November 1975.

The PSOE reappeared as a radical socialist party. The party's programme approved by the 27th Congress in 1976, the first congress held in Madrid since the Second Republic, stated that its goals were 'the supersession of the capitalist mode of production through the conquest of political and economic power, and the socialisation of the means of production, distribution and exchange by the working class'. It also rejected 'any form of accommodation to capitalism, or the simple reform of the system'. In addition, the party defined itself 'as a class party, and therefore a mass party, Marxist and democratic'.

At the same time, however, the party tried to absorb social democrats and win votes on its right. The potential tensions inherent in the attempt to cover such a huge political space were understandably great and typical of the PSOE's history, though they remained subdued in the process of transition towards democracy. But there was a clear clash between the PSOE's image and that of the PCE. From Franco's death in November 1975 to the general elections on 15 June 1977, the question was which of the two parties would occupy the political space of the parliamentary left.

The answer to this question indicated the persistence of political memory over nearly four decades of dictatorship. In the June 1977 elections, the PSOE obtained nearly 28.7 per cent of the vote and became the second largest party — second only to the centre-right coalition of the UCD, the Union of Centre Democrats of President Suarez, which won 33.9 per cent. Proportional representation resulted in the left — PSOE, PCE and PSP — winning 42.2 per cent of the vote and 144 seats out of 350, while the right and centre-right — AP and UCD — won 42.1 per cent of the vote, but 181 seats. The elections showed a strong continuity with the 1936 political cleavages and loyalties. This was despite dramatic changes in the Spanish economy, from a *per capita* income of $200 in 1940 to $2,500 in 1975, despite transformation in Spanish society — 52 per cent of the active population worked in agriculture in 1940, but only 25 per cent in 1975 — and despite virtually 40 years of repressive dictatorship. There is close similarity between the provincial distribution of the Popular Front vote in February 1936 and that of the PSOE-PCE vote in June 1977.

The election results — 9.22 per cent of the vote — were a disappointment for the PCE and did not reflect the extraordinary importance that the communist party had in the underground struggle against Francoism. But the PCE had overestimated its position of hegemony within the left throughout the 1960s, and had not anticipated the powerful socialist resurgence. The geographical distribution of the left vote in the 1977 elections illustrates the extent of competition between the PSOE and the PCE — their electoral constituencies consistently overlapped. The parties, in terms of their electoral attraction, seem to have not been complementary, but competing. Moreover, the PSOE was always strong where the left was strong, whereas the PCE was not always so in the area of heavy left-wing votes. This may suggest the PCE's challenge to the PSOE was not successful in left-wing areas.

The PSOE's electoral strength was increased by the merger with the Popular Socialist Party (PSP) in spring 1978. The PSP share of the 1977 vote was 4.3 per cent, and though the new potential electoral strength of the socialists was not a simple addition of PSOE and PSP, there had been a reinforcement and clarification of the socialist camp which would be likely to contribute to the electoral hegemony of the PSOE in the left. The communist party went further in its process of ideological analysis following the 1977 elections — a process which, notwithstanding its ambiguities, developed the Eurocommunist trend and dropped the Leninist label from official party ideology. After the PCE's ninth congress in April 1978, the new leadership represented a combination of the party's 'old guard' — Ibarruri, Carrillo, Azcarate and Sanchez Montero — and the younger generation of the underground struggle — Sartorius, Ariza, Triana, Saborido and Tamames. The PCE, however, appeared to be in a situation similar to Italy's PSI — unable to find its own political space. The *unified and reduced* ideological spectrum of parliamentary socialism was now occupied electorally by the PSOE.

The PSOE's electoral position, nonetheless, was not quite matched by its trade union strength. Here the persistence of political memory throughout nearly four decades of Francoism was less evident. The Workers' Commissions (CCOO) benefited from their militancy on the shopfloor during the 1960s, obtaining 35.8 per cent of the vote in the trade union elections from January to March 1978. But the UGT resurgence, after its 1960s crisis, should not be underestimated. It won 22.7 per cent of the vote, faring particularly well in large firms.

Two points must be made about the trade union results. First, they refer only to a quarter of the active population and exclude agricultural workers. Second, the Labour Ministry's results, supplied at the last minute, widely contradicted those of the UGT and CCOO, which also showed differences between them. It is obvious that the government, faced with a stiff PSOE parliamentary challenge, was now dealing with an unpalatable alternative — reinforcement of the socialists through UGT, or powerful Workers' Commissions. The Labour Ministry decided to keep relatively obscure what had happened at trade union level. It produced two categories of delegates to the factory councils — 'non-affiliated' and 'independents' — which were ambiguous and could be used to discourage delegates from the Workers' Commissions or the UGT. And both unions claimed many of these 'independent' or 'non-affiliated' delegates for themselves. Further, the elections followed the system of 'open lists' — candidatures not explicitly endorsed by particular trade unions — in firms employing up to 250 workers, and 'closed lists' — candidatures with a trade union label — in larger companies. The 'closed lists' system was defended by the UGT, who hoped to benefit from its historical tradition and socialist image, CCOO supported 'open lists', hoping to gain from the 'militancy without labels' of many of its activists.

It seems the UGT performed better in firms employing more than 250 workers, and CCOO in the smaller units. UGT did well in the Basque Country, particularly Viscaya, the Asturian mines, eastern Andalucia and Old Castile, while the Workers' Commissions were most forceful in Madrid, Catalonia, Valencia and western Andalucia.

The trade union election results have two likely consequences. First, they will strengthen the relationship between the Workers' Commissions and the PCE, as trade union support becomes the main source of strength for the communist party. At the party's ninth Congress, three important trade union leaders — Sartorius, Ariza and Saborido — were promoted to the executive committee. Second, they perpetuate competition between socialists and communists. As the PCE tries to redress the electoral balance in its favour, socialists try and strengthen their trade union support.

Eurocommunism and Democratic Socialism

There are two relevant considerations in comparing Eurocommunist and democratic socialist programmes. The first refers to the nature of the reforms proposed, and the differences in the type of change such reforms would produce. The second question refers to the compatibility between egalitarian policies and pluralism. To what extent can socialism be achieved with a system of electoral competition?

If the nature of the reforms is considered, two points must be noted about the PCE's Eurocommunist programme. First, it is a very gradual programme of reforms, and incorporates an evolutionary conception of the transition to socialism. Gradualism is sometimes defended in terms of what Gramsci called a 'war of position', which would lead to the progressive transformation of the relations of production, and differs from a strategy of 'frontal attacks to Winter Palaces'. Carrillo himself writes that 'the overcoming of social differences will follow a natural process, and will not be the result of coercive measures, but of the development of the productive forces, and of the social services'.[2] The conception of socialism as a process does not eliminate the idea of a 'qualitative step' in the transition to socialism. So a 'new correlation of forces . . . brings about advances . . . through overall structural changes which, at a certain level of accumulation, give rise to a qualitative leap, from the bourgeois to the socialist order'.[3]

The second point is that the characteristics of a socialist economy are nowhere described. Two basic PCE texts in this respect — the report of the 1972 eighth congress and the 1973 manifesto programme — mention only the collective ownership of the fundamental means of production and exchange. The PCE programme is however, much more specific when referring to an intermediate phase of 'social and political democracy'. Here the PCE presents a full programme of reforms: nationalization of sources of finance and large monopolies, land redistribution and reorganisation of agricultural production, tax reforms, maintenance of a private sector — including non-monopolistic industries and small and medium commerce — workers' participation in management of the public and private sector, 'democratic' planning, and policies related to social security, health, urban planning, defence and international relations. In this phase of 'social and political democracy', a mixed economy is therefore accepted, as 'the coexistence of public and private ownership means acceptance of surplus value and the private appropriation of part of this, endorsing the existence of a mixed system. Society has the means to ensure this surplus value is not exorbitant, by means of taxation that is nevertheless sufficient to encourage private enterprise. Moreover, by controlling credit, it has the opportunity to channel savings towards the purposes best suited to the country as a whole'.[4]

The 'social and political democracy' phase is similar to the 'advanced democracy' phase and the 'new stage of the democratic revolution' described respectively by the PCF and the PCI. These allegedly 'intermediate' stages raise two interrelated problems, both due to the absence of a definition of how socialism — what lies beyond the 'qualitative step' — is seen. First, it could be said that these 'intermediate stages' resemble an argument by Zeno of Elsa. For the same reason Achilles could never reach the tortoise, a communist party can never achieve socialism — there would always be intermediate phases. Second, the move from the relatively clear description of what the transitional phase is about to the obscurity of the later stage — socialism — is abandoned to the workings of the 'development of the forces of production'. Eurocommunism, then, does not seem to have a clearer view of socialism, and of the socialist transition, than parliamentary socialist parties upholding programmes of radical reform. The only difference seems to be the mystifying belief in an evolutionary phase, situated in the indefinite future.

The PSOE presents a programme of transition that is patently a 'revolutionary reformist' project, indeed similar to that of the PCE, except for its greater explicitness on nationalisation, and the form of planning and democratic management of the economy. The PSOE's 1976 programme included nationalisation of the 10 largest banks, controlling 80 per cent of the sector's total resources, and 25 per cent of the 200 biggest industrial corporations. Further nationalisation was sought in electricity, oil exploration and refining, coal, natural gas, nuclear energy, steel, pharmaceutical production and food, extending to the public sector, which today covers 27 of the top 200 industrial companies, 70 per cent of the added value produced by the largest industrial firms, 25 per cent of GDP and 50 per cent of total industrial investment. The PSOE also discusses in its programme measures to avoid economic collapse after a left-wing electoral victory, precipitated by a flight of capital, an investment crisis and growing inflation.[5] The party says it does not offer 'a simple catalogue of repairs to the facade of the capitalist building'.[6]

The PSOE strategy was presented as a dialectical method of transition to socialism, which will combine the parliamentary struggle with popular mobilisation . . . setting up democratic organs of power at the base — co-operatives, neighbourhood associations, village and district committees — that seek to deepen the concept of democracy, overcoming the formal character that political freedoms have in the capitalist state'. And the party states that 'the degree of pressure to be applied must be in relation to the resistance presented by the bourgeoisie to the democratic rights of the people, and logically we do not exclude those acts of force that will be necessary'.[7] There is a clear similarity between the strategy of hegemony, at the level of 'civil society', followed by the PCI, and the PSOE's strategy of a 'progressive conquest of parcels of political and social power', 'deepening of democracy and progressive enlargement of the limits of freedoms', decentralisation of power, popular control of areas of collective life, extension of political consciousness such that 'the majority of citizens objectively interested in the construction of a socialist society becomes a subjectively conscious political majority'.[8] There is clearly a strong similarity between the PSOE ideology and strategy and that of Eurocommunist programmes. This convergence was accepted by socialist leaders, who argued that 'the evolution of communist parties, and of the PCE in particular, justifies the socialists in their positions of 1921 . . . The communists come to join a traditional strategy of socialists in general, and of the PSOE in particular'.[9]

Examining the PCE's conception of pluralism, two aspects seem particularly relevant. The first is that despite the title of Carrillo's book, there is no explicit theory of the state in the PCE. It seems that the state is seen as an instrument for reform, able to be 'used' to implement cumulative reforms, but in executing them, it would be gradually changing and modifying its class basis. Occasional contradictions do emerge, though — for instance, when Carrillo criticises state socialist societies for failing to achieve Lenin's goal of 'smashing' the state.[10]

The second aspect of the PCE's pluralist conception refers to its commitment to democracy. The party states repeatedly that it will defend pluralism, cultural and ideological freedom and democratic rights, not only in the access to power, but also in the transition to socialism and in the socialist society itself. The party says: 'We do not conceive the future socialist system in Spain as a single party system . . . but as a democratic multi-party system . . . A free and open ideological struggle will take place, even among close socialist forces.' Carrillo argues that democracy is a historical, universal achievement which can never be surrendered.[11] Yet there are also some apparent contradictions in the party's democratic commitment. The PCE has defended the Bolshevik revolution in the historical context of Russia in 1917, and Carrillo insistently criticises Kautsky's position against Lenin. A more general point is made that in underdeveloped, capitalist countries the pluralist democratic struggle makes no sense. This culturally relativist view of democracy seems to correspond to the reactionary view that underdeveloped countries are not 'ripe' for democracy, and introduces into Eurocommunism's democratic commitment a smack of opportunism. Also Carrillo makes vague reference to hypothetical situations in which a democratically elected government might be brought down by political strikes because it would not conform to the 'wishes of the masses'. Just how these wishes are to be assessed, and what gives this action legitimacy against an electoral mandate, are questions which remain obscure.[12]

The difficulties of reconciling socialist programmes and political pluralism have been lucidly analysed by Parkin.[13] If Eurocommunism sees socialism as a process, is it possible to accept setbacks in that process, and for how long? Pluralism and electoral competition would normally transform such a process into something like Penelope's endless weaving and unravelling — with no Odysseus coming after 20 years of progression and retrogression. Eurocommunism argues that a growing 'hegemony' at the 'civil society' level would eventually produce an 'irreversible' situation. But is it really possible to believe that people's minds will eventually converge on a stable, socialist ideology? The PCE seems to believe this. The central committee report to the PCE's eighth congress in 1972 said 'the dictatorship of the revolutionary socialist forces, supported by laws and institutions geared to defend collective social ownership, to stimulate the development of society towards increasingly advanced socialist forms, towards communism, may be exerted, while assuring formal democratic freedoms to the bourgeois opposition, until the latter becomes an obsolete anachronism and fades away by itself for lack of an economic, social or ideological basis'. But this leads to a strange and unconvincing conclusion. Pluralism would be protected, though it would eventually be superseded by a decrease in ideological differentiation — a growing similarity of class interests, following an increasingly common class situation. A problem, of course, is what would happen to these beliefs if successive reformist attempts by a Eurocommunist party in government should fail, and be followed by the election of conservative governments and U-turns in the process of socialism? To what extent are the conception of socialism as a process and the pluralist commitment compatible?

Both in terms of the 'political economy of the transition', or the programme of radical cumulative reforms, and in terms of the compatibility of egalitarianism and pluralism, or socialism as a process and the limitations of the electoral mandate, the PCE's Eurocommunism is riddled with difficulties and obscurities. Does it see a mixed economy as compatible with socialism? Where is the dividing line between the transitional stage of 'social and political democracy' and socialism? What reforms can go beyond a reformist management of capitalism? To what extent is socialism, both as a process and a type of society, compatible with electoral competition? Is democracy a relative value? And, if it is, in what circumstances does Eurocommunism accept other political arrangements as legitimate? Eurocommunism does not answer these questions. It tends to protect itself behind what it calls 'the concrete analysis of concrete situations' — a euphemism for *ad hoc*, ideological-theoretical opportunism.

The two problems of the programme of 'revolutionary reforms', the political economy of the transition, and of the contradictory relationship between pluralism and egalitarianism, are equally difficult for democratic socialism in general. In that sense it seems that there has been an increasingly homogenous problematic within the parliamentary left. The PCL, the PSOE, the PCE, the PSF, the left of the Labour Party, are all in a similar perplexing situation. And criticisms of the positions of these parliamentary socialist groups seem to present an alternative only when representative democracy is rejected. Only then is it possible to believe that a different image of society is being proposed. This may be the reason why the critique of Eurocommunism made by Claudin[14] — based fundamentally on the persistent defence of state socialist societies by Eurocommunist parties, and on the moderation and gradualism of Eurocommunist programmes — is ultimately unconvincing. Claudin does not even suggest an alternative programme of reform and transition which would bring the 'qualitative leap' any closer. His proposal for a strategy combining a parliamentary and extra-parliamentary struggle does not solve the problem of right-wing backlashes, economic boycotts and electoral defeats. Nor does his argument that representative democracy must be complemented by democracy at the 'grass roots' have much specific content. He, too, sees democracy as a relative value, declaring that when the proletariat is a minority and the level of development of the forces of production is low, universal suffrage can be replaced by violence. And so in January 1918 the Bolsheviks had the legitimacy to dissolve the constituent assembly in Russia.[15] Neither the economic nor the political difficulties of democratic socialism are satisfactorily analysed by Claudin.

Apart from Stalinism and Cold War dilemmas, democratic socialism is, to a great extent, back to the general problem of German social democracy before 1914. Carrillo's insistent attack on Kautsky concentrates on his view of the Bolshevik revolution. But it does not face the central issue that German social democracy, in its Marxist period, believed in the reformist potential of the state, conceived the transition to socialism as being only possible through democratic means, and thought capitalism's structural contradictions would eventually lead to socialist change. It could plausibly be said that since then democratic socialist parties have learnt more about what to avoid than about what to do. This uncertainty was spectacularly shown in the dispute within the Union of the Left at the French general election in March 1978. The alternative to social democratic, accommodative reformism and undemocratic leftism has not yet been clearly formulated. In this situation of greater ideological homogeneity and the common problematic of the parliamentary left, what democratic socialists and communist parties have to offer is very similar. Yet, paradoxically, when electoral and/or trade union strength is divided between socialist and communist parties, the result may easily be bitter competition for this unified political space.

4 EUROCOMMUNISM: CONCLUSIONS

The former Foreign Secretary, Dr David Owen, said in his Hugh Anderson memorial lecture in 1978, that we 'should give no currency' to the term Eurocommunism because 'it tends to make people suspend their critical faculties, avoid analysing the phenomenon seriously, country by country, and instead take refuge in generalities'.

This pamphlet, in fact, has approached the problem 'country by country' and has subjected the three major Eurocommunist parties — those of Italy, France and Spain — to a critical analysis. This has often led to emphasis on the differences between the parties and the national contexts in which they operate.

Yet certain common themes have emerged. We have noted that all the parties known as 'eurocommunist', while continuing to use the name 'communist' and claiming continuity with parties founded in the wake of the Russian revolution as sections of the Communist International, nonetheless categorically reject both the model of the Russian revolution and the international discipline which was the raison d'etre of the Comintern. While for the most part accepting that Soviet society is, in some sense, 'socialist' — though Carrillo has questioned even this — they insist the 'socialism' they wish to build in their own countries is completely different from what exists today in the Soviet Union and eastern Europe. They also insist on the right of each communist party to form its own policies in total independence from Moscow, or any other capital with pretensions to a 'guiding role'.

This is an important difference from the immediate post-war period, when communist parties in both western and eastern Europe already proclaimed, as Eurocommunists do today, they were following a peaceful road to socialism, different from the violent seizure of power by the bolsheviks in 1917. For at that time they continued to describe the society resulting from the Russian bolshevik revolution as democratic and admirable. The difference was not in the objective, but only in the path chosen to reach it. Today it is the validity of Soviet 'socialism' as a goal which is openly rejected. The Eurocommunists not only reject it as a model for their own countries, but also point out its inability to solve the problems of the countries where it is practised, and the resultant injustices and hardships suffered by Russians and other east Europeans. Such criticisms were unheard of in the communist parties of 1944-47, when there was never the slightest public questioning of the leadership provided for progressive and democratic forces throughout the world by 'le génial Staline'.

Eurocommunism is essentially a process by which communist parties — not only in Italy, Spain and France, but also in Scandinavia, Switzerland, Belgium, Australia, Japan, and here in Britain — seek to adapt themselves to the realities of political life in modern western democracies, and to dissociate themselves from a Soviet model which now has neither attraction nor relevance for the mass of working people in western countries. It is not a system or a doctrine, but a rather ill-defined corpus of ideas, improvised over a period of years by leaders of already established parties, acting and speaking under a wide variety of political pressures.

Of course, these leaders were communists long before they were Eurocommunists, and they insist there is no contradiction between the two. Implicitly, at least, they are claiming to be *better* communists than Brezhnev and his crew. What do they mean by communism, then? Essentially, it seems, a continued, long-term commitment to abolishing capitalism and exploitation of man by man, to creation of a classless society in which the means of production, distribution and exchange will be owned in common. But do not we, as democratic socialists, have the same commitment? What has traditionally divided us from communists has been that we were pledged to bring about this fundamental social change only by mobilising the explicit support of the majority of the population, whereas they believed that they had the right and the duty to seize power and impose the change as a conscious minority, the 'vanguard of the working class'. If Eurocommunists have genuinely renounced this pretention, the argument has, in effect, been resolved in our favour. Should the great split of 1919-21 in western European socialist parties not now be healed, with communists and socialists rejoining each other in a united and powerful labour movement?

Logically, perhaps, they should, and it is possible that over the next generation that will indeed be the result. But the mutual hostility and suspicions accumulated during half a century of bitter rivalry make it unlikely to happen quickly. Communist parties, including Eurocommunists, still have great difficulty in accepting that Socialist International parties are genuinely representative of the working class in their respective countries, or genuinely interested in giving the working class real power. They still tend to see themselves as the principal, if not the only genuine expression of working class aspirations. If they value socialist parties as allies, it is mainly for their ability to mobilise sections of society beyond the hard core of manual workers in manufacturing industry, thereby bringing about a broad alliance against monopoly capital. But it is an alliance in which the communists, as, in their own eyes, the true representatives of the hard core working class, still expect to play the leading or 'hegemonic' role. If they fear socialist parties as enemies, it is because they see them as capable of leading astray at least a section of the working class into class collaboration policies — a kind of capitalist fifth-column within the labour movement, whose role is to salvage capitalist interests at times when the crisis has become so acute as to make it impossible for parties with an overtly capitalist ideology to remain in power on their own.

Few of us could deny that the behaviour of socialist parties in office in various west European countries since the war has given a certain plausibility to this charge. Dr Owen was surely right to say that the continued, and in some cases expanding, appeal of communism in western Europe is 'built on dissatisfaction with existing European political parties, the failure to tackle serious defects in our society, high unemployment, gross inequalities of wealth and power', and to see this as an extremely serious challenge to democratic socialism. But if communists have solid reasons to remain suspicious of social democrats, we, too, as democratic socialists, have good grounds for hesitating before taking at face value the Eurocommunists' protestations of conversion to democracy. The issue is not so much one of their sincerity as of their understanding of what democracy is, and also of their priorities. Our own suspicions are sometimes sharpened by the very efforts which Eurocommunists make to allay the suspicions of other parties to our right.

Are they not embarking on precisely those policies of class collaboration for which social democrats have been condemned, often rightly, in the past? How much confidence can one have in the promises of parties which display such astonishing tactical flexibility? Indeed, are Eurocommunists seriously interested in building an alliance capable of winning majority support for socialist transformation? Such an alliance should surely offer itself as a clear and preferable alternative to the existing capitalist order, and the parties identified with it, whereas — at least in Italy and Spain — the CPs have been more preoccupied with getting themselves accepted as legitimate participants in conventional politics, even as partners, by the capitalists themselves and the other political and social forces associated with the existing order, both nationally and internationally — the Catholic church, armed forces, the United States. governments of other West European countries, and, in Spain, the monarchy. Even in France, where the PCF did seem to have dedicated itself wholeheartedly over a long period to the construction of a left-wing alternative, its behaviour over the last year has left many observers with the impression that its leaders considered it more important to dominate the left than to defeat the right.

An essential part of Eurocommunism is acceptance of the idea of alternation in power — the idea that government and opposition can change places as the result of an election. Yet though they accept it in theory, the Eurocommunist parties still do not appear convinced that things will happen like that in practice. Whether or not they themselves are sincere in promising to relinquish power should they be defeated in an election after obtaining it, it is increasingly clear that they do not think it realistic to expect their opponents to hand over power to them without a fight — a fight which, in the circumstances of western Europe, communists would be most unlikely to win.

The communists' conclusion seems to be, at least as far as the PCI is concerned, 'if you can't lick 'em, join 'em'. The Italian, and, so far, on a more limited scale, Spanish communists, are saying to the establishments of their respective countries, of the European community and of the western alliance: 'All right, we understand that you are not willing to trust us as adversaries. But please accept us as partners. We are anxious to make our contribution to solving the economic crisis and strengthening democracy.' As an earnest of their good faith, Italian communists go out of their way to consult and co-operate with Christian Democrats and other 'bourgeois' parties in local government — even in areas where there is a clear left-wing majority. This behaviour is not necessarily reassuring to democratic socialists. Rather than a free choice between left and right, it seems to foreshadow a process whereby both left and right will be spared the risk of electoral defeat because they will confront the electorate in alliance, and a system in which any real opposition, whether from left or right, will be frowned on as irresponsible and extremist. To a considerable degree this seems already to be the PCI's attitude. Its treatment of the Radical Party is particularly instructive in this respect.

For all these reasons, it seems the question of formal links between democratic socialist and Eurocommunist parties is at least premature. The question of a political alliance to struggle for socialist transformation by democratic means is clearly crucial in those countries where Eurocommunist parties are strong. But it is unfortunately one to which the Eurocommunist parties themselves have yet to give a satisfactory answer. The socialist parties in those countries therefore face a difficult situation, to which each has to compose its own response. The guiding principle, though, must surely be that the more convincing the programme for socialist change the socialist parties put forward, the harder it will be for the communist parties to refuse their co-operation without losing credibility with their own supporters. The same principle applies in Britain, but here, of course, the co-operation or non co-operation of the Communist Party is a matter of far less importance. We need a convincing socialist programme for its own sake.

The question is, do we have one? Indeed, can any socialist programme any longer be convincing within the context of one country? The present crisis affects the whole of the industrialised capitalist world. It is doubtful whether a country of Britain's size — especially one in which foreign trade and investment is traditionally so important — provides an economic space in which a socialist solution could be applied with any hope of success. Solutions need to be put forward at least on the scale of Western Europe, and are likely to emerge only from a dialogue in which all the important socialist forces of Western Europe take part. We can hardly deny a place among those forces to the communist parties of Italy, France and Spain. Certainly, our socialist comrades in those countries would not do this, despite their many reservations about the validity of Eurocommunism as a democratic socialist formula. The problem is not at this stage one of formal links or alliances, but of a common effort to define attainable socialist objectives in western Europe and a strategy for achieving them. This is why a dialogue between socialists and communists in western Europe today is now so important.

FOOTNOTES
1 J M Maravall, *Dictatorship and Political Dissent,* London, Tavistock, 1978, chapters 2, 3 and 4.
2 Santiago Carrillo, *Eurocommunism and the State,* Lawrence and Wishart, 1977, p 80.
3 *Op cit*, p 83.
4 *Op cit*, p 80.
5 *Programme of Transition,* XXVII Congreso del Partido Socialista Obrero Espanol, Barcelona, Avance, 1977, pp 159-324.

6 *Ibid*, p 208.
7 *Ibid*, p 117.
8 PSOE's *Democracia y Socialismo en el Sur de Europa*, Madrid, 1977, pp 50, 52, 53.
9 F Bustelo, G Peces Barba, C de Vicente, V Zapatero, *Partido Socialista Obrero Espanol*, Barcelona, Avance, 1976, p 93.
10 Carrillo, *op cit*, p 156.
11 Carrillo, *op cit*, p 12.
12 Carrillo, *Eurocommunism and the State, op cit*, pp 98, 99, 152.
13 F Parkin, *Class, Inequality and Political Order,* London, MacGibbon and Kee, 1971, chapters 4, 6.
14 F Claudin, *Eurocommunism y Socialismo,* Madrid, Siglo XXI, 1977.
15 F Claudin, *op cit*.

Now read Labour's other Background Papers

SENSE ABOUT DEFENCE

The Report of the Labour Party
Defence Study Group

95p

COLD PEACE

Soviet Power and Western
Security

60p

From: Literature Sales
The Labour Party
144/152 Walworth Rd
SE17 1JT   01-703 0833

Labour Weekly

LABOUR'S OWN NEWSPAPER

PICTURE: ANDREW WIARD (REPORT)